Thriving on Plant Based Food Storage

Food Stroage Philly Pizza (page 94)

Raw food recipes highlighting dried fruits and vegetables

By Kachina Choate
Summer Bear

Thriving on Plant Based Food Storage
Raw food recipes highlighting dried fruits and vegetables

Copyright © 2020 Kachina Choate

All rights reserved. No part of this publication may be reproduced, stored in a retrieval system, or transmitted in any form or by any means, electronic, mechanical, photocopying, recording, or other- wise, without the prior written consent of the copyright owner. dollkachina@gmail.com

First Edition 2008 Second Edition 2020

Kachina Choate Summer Bear
Thriving on Plant Based Food Storage Raw food recipes highlighting dried fruits and vegetables

ISBN: 978-1-938142-06-2 (print)
ISBN: 978-1-938142-07-9 (ebook)

1. Raw Foods 2. Cookery (Natural foods) 3. Food Storage 4 Vegetarian Food

Editor: Karie Clingo

This book does not intend to cure or give medical advice. We want to educate, inform, and empower readers to make their own decisions on their health and well being. Each person might have different reactions to changes in diet. If you have concerns about your health or nutrition, consult your healthcare advisor.

Brownie (page 123) with Almond Butter and Carob Frosting (page 127)

CONTENTS

Peach Mint Lemonade (page 56)

Sprout Soup (page 83)

Fudge (page 128)

4 INTRODUCTION

5 WHY STORE FOOD?

6 FOOD STORAGE MISHAPS

9 WATER STORAGE

12 WHAT TO STORE

19 HOW TO STORE

27 FOOD STORAGE AND OTHER INFORMATION

31 GARDENING

37 EQUIPMENT

39 MENU IDEAS

54 JUST ADD WATER RECIPES

71 FOOD STORAGE RECIPES

134 ROOT CELLR RECIPES

140 YOUR RECIPES

Introduction

A common misconception is that you can't store raw food when a disaster strikes and have to eat what is available. I wrote this book to show how it's possible to store raw foods now--and for the future.

The best time to prepare for a disaster is BEFORE one happens. It has been said that if you are prepared, you shall not fear. And it's hard to know exactly when an emergency will strike--now is the time to plan and store the food you will need!

I hope this book will help you be confident, make a plan, get started now for any situation, and enjoy a long-term plant-based diet, and in the meantime, save money and have peace of mind. The most important thing to remember is to do your best now--and store what you can! Start with doing something this week!

Joseph rules Egypt - bible drawing by Otto Semler

Chapter 1 Why Store Food?

And let them gather all the food of those good years that come, and lay up corn under the hand of Pharaoh, and let them keep food in the cities.

*And when all the land of Egypt was famished, the people cried to Pharaoh for bread...
And Joseph opened all the storehouses.*

- Genesis Chapter 41 verses 35 and 55-56

Like Joseph of Egypt, whose inspired food storing saved Egypt from starvation. You can also store food for yourself and family.

Almost every society, human and animal, store food, and yet the average American household has less than a week's supply of food on hand.

Without being paranoid or panicked, there are many important reasons to put the extra food away, such as to:

- Prepare for unexpected periods of scarcity or famine.
- Take advantage of short-term food surplus, during harvest or times of plenty.
- Establish better dietary balance throughout the year.
- Prepare for catastrophes, emergencies, or disasters.
- Plan for financial difficulties such as loss of job or government shutdown.
- Ensure food accessibility when you are unable to secure items from stores.
- Remain self-sufficient by being able to provide for yourself and family in times of need.

Some people feel it is unnecessary to prepare for emergencies and assume that disaster organizations--or churches--will rush to their rescue and feed them.

Most governing agencies advise, preparing "at least a three

day supply of non-perishable food." While securing three days' supply is an excellent place to start, disasters and devastating events could last for months--or even years. It is just not possible for federal and state organizations to provide all of our food and water. So, being prepared and as self-sufficient as possible makes sense. It may alleviate significant suffering for you and your family.

Food storage is a form of insurance to protect your family from the unexpected. It is comforting to know you have food during natural disasters, but it can also buffer any lean financial times. If the stores or markets are closed--and money isn't available--you can have greater peace of mind--knowing that you and your family will not go hungry.

Chapter 2 Food Storage Mishaps Learned the Hard Way

Be wise as you store food and water. Rather than going to extremes or debt to establish your food storage, you can carefully plan over time to build your home storage. Just begin by adding a few items in your cart during regular grocery shopping, and soon you will have food storage.

Mishap #1
Not storing what you eat.

"If you won't eat it now, what makes you think you will eat it later?" -Gaye Levy of Backdoor Survival

One way to make sure your family eats what you store is to store your family's favorite foods. It is also useful to introduce dried and freeze-dried foods into the diet so that they won't be strange to the digestion. Keep food storage meals in rotation as part of your regular menu plan.

Mishap #2
Not having a wide enough variety of foods stored.

There was a time I thought I had plenty of food storage because I had lots of nuts. After living on food storage for two weeks, I found that I missed fresh fruits and vegetables and got tired of nuts. I learned I needed to store a lot more dried fruits, vegetables, and seeds to sprouts for variety. Sprouts are your ultimate source of fresh greens, especially in the winter. During a crisis is not the time to change your diet. We get bored and want to eat different foods, so store more than just basics. If you need to live off your food storage, you'll be much happier with a wide variety of food for a couple of months rather than a year's supply of a few items.

Mishap #3
Using incorrect or unmanageable storage containers.

Lots of food gets thrown away because it is improperly stored—store foods in BPH free food-grade plastic containers. If you store food in glass, remember it can break.

Do not store food unsealed or with twist ties bags, as they become susceptible to moisture, insects, and rodents. Never use trash can liners to store food; they get treated with pesticides. Food can absorb harmful chemicals that may cause severe illness or adverse reactions.

Avoid unmanageable containers that are too big to handle or, when opened, would be too much for your family to eat quickly. Choose containers that are easy to handle, pest-proof, and moisture safe. Consider storing food in serving sizes for you and your family. First, remove the air, seal, and then place the servings into a food-grade bucket for storage. During a short-term emergency, you can pull out what you need without repackaging the food.

NOTE: Never reuse containers that once held toxic chemicals!

Mishap #4
Not knowing how to use your storage.

Know how to use the equipment and foods you store. A disaster may not be the right time to learn if you have never used a wheat grinder or sprouted whole wheat.

Make recipes now from your food storage. I strongly suggest that you try to live off your food storage for a week or two to see if you are storing what you need. Look through recipe books and see what you can make out of food storage--and plan your shopping accordingly.

Have fun as you plan your storage, experiment with a friend. Host a potluck where everyone brings a dish from his or her food storage and share ideas and recipes. Please feel free to share any thoughts, experiences, and new recipes you come up with on my social media pages. I would love to see them!

Mishap #5
Not storing enough water

When using dehydrated foods, you will need to store more water. Use the water to rehydrate fruit, vegetables, powdered fruit juice, and other types of food preparation.

Do not drink the water used to soak nuts and seeds. As they absorb the water, nuts and seeds release enzyme inhibitors into the water. Instead, use this water for cleaning or watering plants.

Mistake #6
Not rotating or updating storage.

Some people secure their food storage and then forget about it. The problem is food needs to be rotated and enjoyed. Some foods spoil faster than others. Label everything with the purchase date. You can keep a log or notebook with expiration dates to know what needs to be rotated and replaced.

Mishap #7
Storing everything in one place.

In 2005, a flood in St. George, Utah, took out part of a home in the rushing waters, and their food storage all disappeared downstream. Think about disaster risks where you live and plan your storage locations accordingly, put it into multiple places in your home, garage, in your car, and so forth.

Mishap #8
Forgetting to prepare for your pets need.

When planning your food storage, don't forget your pets! They will need to eat and drink water, just like the rest of the family.

Image from
'What I Learned from my Deaf Cat'
by Kachina and Berndine Choate

Chapter 3 Water Storage

Both oxygen and water are vital to the human body. A person may live for weeks or even months without food but will die in a matter of days without adequate water. Generally, the human body needs four times as much water as food. For every pound of food you eat, you should drink four pounds of water (about half a gallon).

Water is comparatively inexpensive to store, and now is the time to save it. Water that we use when life is normal becomes critical in an emergency. Most people use 140 gallons a day for drinking, bathing, dishes, laundry, etc. if you have the room, store more water than you think you might need.

The minimum amount of water suggested for two weeks is fourteen gallons per person and pet. In other words; two quarts of water for drinking and two quarts for food preparation and sanitation daily. Those who are in high altitude or dry climates will need more. Those that need more water are the elderly, infirmed, nursing mothers, and people that physically exert themselves.

When it comes to water, the more you have, the merrier and cleaner you will be. Remember that if you are using water to soak nuts, rehydrate food, and sprout seeds, your water use will be at least double per person, not including sanitation water. Which means you would need a minimum of 28 gallons per person for two weeks. You can drink water used to rehydrate fruits and vegetables. It becomes flavored water.

Choose water containers that are food-grade, clean, and opaque, where light cannot penetrate. Look for the "HDPE" High-Density Polyethylene and "2" label on containers for safe, long-term storage.

If your water is bacteria-free when you store it, you probably don't need to treat it further. Bacteria-free water, stored in clean containers, will stay safe for several years. Store your water in cool, dark, and dry areas.

We recommended rotating your water every six months. Use commercially bottled water by the expiration date. Check containers yearly and replace the water as necessary. If there are no leaks or contamination, stored water lasts for five years or longer without rotation. However, it is a good idea to check your water for purity and taste periodically.

The bulk of your water can be in 55 gallons, polyethylene (plastic) water drums, found in most food storage or local container companies. Remember that water is heavy and it is hard to move.

You can also use food-grade, quality containers for water. You can often get food-grade water containers from companies that distribute beverages or syrups. Which, when cleaned well, can provide a less expensive, perfectly fine storage container for your water.

NOTE: the taste or odor of the previous contents may leach into the plastic with time. If you plan to reuse containers for water, make sure the previous flavors are something you wouldn't mind tasting in your water. Never use storage containers used to store toxic products. Milk or juice containers retain proteins, bacteria, and sugars that can contaminate water.

Tips to remember about water containers are:

DO NOT store water in glass or metal because of breakage and rust.

DO NOT store water in milk jugs. They break down and become brittle.

DO NOT store water in containers that held any hazardous chemicals.

To store water, fill the bottle to the top and seal the container with the original cap. Full containers keep lid gaskets moist and maintain an airtight seal.

Writing the fill date on the outside of the container helps with proper rotation. As water sits, oxidation can affect the taste of stored water or 'goes flat.' Improve the taste by pouring the water back and forth between containers to refresh it or beat it with a hand-held eggbeater.

Water weighs approximately eight pounds per gallon. A 55-gallon filled water drum would weigh about 440 pounds, which is too heavy and awkward to carry while smaller containers hold less water and would require more trips to get the water needed, especially if you have to go on foot. I recommend that you have a variety of sizes of containers. If you have the room, store large containers along with smaller containers that you can handle.

Another good idea is to have a reliable water purification system. Numerous disinfectant techniques include:

SOLAR HEAT:

One commonly used and inexpensive method is solar disinfection. Place water in a food-grade bottle then put the water in direct sunlight for least six hours. If the day is cloudy, then it will take a minimum of two days to disinfect.

BOILING:

To clean water by boiling is a well-established way of purifying water. Place water in a pot and bring to a boil for 5-10 minutes and cool. Use a filter to remove all solid particles, especially if the water came from doubtful water sources.

CHEMICALS:

Iodine and chlorine belong to the same halogen group and share the common property of being oxidants. Different halogens vary in their oxidation potential and disinfection power. Since the early 1900s,

Iodine-based disinfection of water for potable water treatment is done by using iodine tablets or adding five drops of liquid iodine per quarter of water. Iodine is more stable than chlorine and quite effective in treating giardia.

For more than 100 years, **chlorine** has been an effective way to purify water. Use six drops of unscented chlorine--per gallon of water-- and let the water stand for at least 30 minutes before drinking. In water, chlorine treats viruses, bacteria, and parasites.

WATER FILTERS:

Activated carbon filters known as carbon filters are generally responsible for removing larger particles like sediment and silt from your water. They work by attracting and absorbing particles until they are no longer present in the water. Because carbon filters reduce the amount of chlorine and other contaminants, they can help water taste better.

Reverse osmosis filters remove all sorts of contaminants and improves the taste of water. Developed initially to separate seawater from salt, it purifies through pressure it to force water through a membrane where contaminants cannot follow.

Alkaline/Water Ionizers use electrolysis where water passes over electrically charged plates and then separates into two streams. One stream is alkaline, and the other is acidic.

One of the newest filtering technologies is **UV Filters**. Ultraviolet radiation can destroy various bacteria. UV systems terminate 99.99% of harmful microorganisms without adding chemicals or changing your water's taste or odor.

UV light looks similar to a small flashlight. Just swish the wand around in the water for a few minutes to kill the bacteria. Just remember the solid particles in the water are not filtered. Using reverse osmosis system--or carbon block filters removes those particles.

If you want a more environmentally friendly way of purifying your water, this filter may well be the answer because it doesn't need any chemicals or additional heat to be effective.

These are just a few of the water purification systems available on the market. Choose the method that you are most comfortable using and can afford, and have a backup plan--just in case. Do your research and see which systems work the best for you.

Chapter 4 What to Store

The best way to know what to store is to understand what you eat. Keep a log of all the food and the amounts used in a week or a month. The amount will vary for each person and family.

To figure out how much you need, keep track of the pounds of fresh fruits and vegetables used. You will want to store that amount in dried equivalents.

Keep track of how much water you use for soaking, sprouting, and drinking. You will want to store at least this much. Make sure you can purify local water.

NOTE: Take advantage of discounted fresh fruits and vegetables when it is in season, buy more and dry it. I prepare the same food using a variety of methods such as diced, pureed, sliced, chopped, dried, then powdered, etc. Please rotate all items as you usually would.

Basic Food Storage Ideas

FRUITS,
Dried and/or Freeze Dried

Apples
Apricots
Bananas
Berries
Cherries
Coconut
Cranberry
Grapefruit
Lemon
Lime
Mango
Orange
Papaya
Peaches
Pears
Pineapple
Plums
Raspberries
Strawberries
Sun-Dried Olives
Watermelon
and other available fruits.

VEGETABLES
Dried and/or Freeze Dried:

Anaheim Peppers
Artichokes Hearts
    (Optional Not a Raw Product)
Bell Peppers
    (Red, Yellow, Orange)
Broccoli
Cabbage
Carrots
Cauliflower
Celery
Corn
Cucumber
Garlic
Green Beans
Hot Peppers
Kale
Mushrooms
Onion
Peas
Pumpkin
Spinach
Sun-Dried Olives
Sweet Potato
Tomatoes
Variety of Summer Squash
Variety of Winter Squash
Zucchini--and any other vegetables that appeal to you.

ROOT CELLAR: (see page 24)

Apples
Beets
Butternut Squash
Carrots
Garlic
Jicama
Large Yams
Parsnips
Pumpkin
Rutabaga
Sweet Potato
Turnips
Winter Squash

Note: Do not store apples with other fruits/vegetables as gasses promote over-ripening

SEEDS and NUTS:

Almonds
Brazil Nuts
Cashews Nuts
Garbanzo Beans
Gold and Brown Flax
Hazelnuts
Macadamia Nuts

Pecans
Pine Nuts
Pumpkin Seeds
Sesame Seeds
Sunflower Seeds
Walnuts
Other Nuts

NUT/SEED BUTTERS:

Almond Butter
Tahini (Sesame Seed Butter)
Caoco Butter

OIL:

Olive Oil
Avocado Oil
Grape Seed Oil
Coconut Oil
Others

It is essential to rotate oils. Choose cold-pressed or unrefined oils--non-GMO and organic. Oils that need to be refrigerated are not suitable for long-term storage since you may not have access to refrigeration in an emergency

SWEETENERS:

Coconut Nectar
Raw Coconut Sugar
Raw Honey
Raw Agave
Raisins
Dates
Fresh Dried Stevia Leaves
Dried Fruit reconstituted with water.

SEASONINGS:
Store those you use.

Allspice
Basil
Black Pepper
Caraway Seeds
Cardamom Seeds
Cayenne Pepper
Celery Seed
Chili Powder
Chives
Cilantro
Cinnamon
Cloves
Coriander
Crushed Red Pepper
Cumin Seed
Curry Powder
Dill
Garlic Powder
Garlic Salt
Ginger
Himalayan Crystal Salt
Italian Seasoning
Kelp
Lovage
Marjoram
Mexican Seasoning
Mustard Seeds
Mustard Seed Powder
Nutmeg
Onion Powder
Oregano
Paprika
Parsley
Pizza Seasoning
Poppy Seeds
Poultry Seasoning
Pumpkin Pie Spice
Red Chili Pepper
Rosemary
Sage
Savory
Slippery Elm Powder
Thyme
Turmeric Powder
Vanilla, Bean
Vanilla, Pure Extract
White Pepper
Others you commonly use

GRAINS:
(I sprout and grow my grains into grass for juice)

Buckwheat
Kamut (Wheat Berries)
Oat Groats
Rye Berries
Wild Rice, Black
Quinoa

BEANS: (For sprouting)

Adzuki Beans
Black-Eyed Peas,
Chickpeas
Mung Bean, Spouts
and others

SPROUTS:

Garden/Sprouting Seeds:
Alfalfa
Baby Arugula
Basil
Chia Seeds
Chives
Dill
Lentils

Microgreens:
Mint
Parsley
Peas
Radishes
Shallots
Sunflower
Triticale
Sproutable Wheat

Other Items:

Cacao Nibs
Coconut, Unsweetened
Nutritional Yeast
Raw Carob Powder
Raw Apple Cider Vinegar
Raw Coconut Flour
Hibiscus Flowers

HELPFUL TOOLS:

Dehydrator
Sun Dehydrator
Manual Hand Blender
Sprouting Equipment
Spiralizer
Manual Bicycle Blender
Manual Juicer
Wheat Grass Juicer
Generator
Solar Generator

TIP 1: Know how your manual equipment works and how much water it takes to clean. If it takes 3 gallons to clean, it will not be practical when water is in short supply.

TIP 2: When you buy one item, remove the one from food storage and replace it with the one you purchased--placing the new one in the back of the row, using the oldest first.

TIP 3: At the farmer's market, buy double the amount, one to eat and one to dry.

There is no need to panic and feel like you need to buy everything at once. By purchasing a little extra every time, you have a chance, you can expand and stock up quite naturally to thrive in a time of need. You may be surprised how quickly you can build your storage.

Some of the essential things to store include:

- Water – at least one gallon of water per person per day.
- Dried or freeze-dried food–the bare minimum is three days' worth.

By looking at what you already use, you can know what you need.

Sample of Annual Breakdown to Build Food Storage

MONTH ONE

- 1 gallon of water per person and pets
- 1 jar of nut butter
- 1 large can dry fruit/vegetables.
- 2 bags of sprouting seeds (see list)
- 1 bag of Kamut or other wheat berries
- Hand-operated can opener
- Dry at least one tray of garden vegetables and fruits.
- Complete an assessment of your food needs and the resources you already have on hand--or need to acquire.
- Date each perishable food item with a permanent marking pen.

MONTH TWO

- 1 gallon of water per person and pets
- oil (of choice)
- 2 seasonings (of choice)
- pet food,
- baby food, if needed
- dry at least one tray of garden vegetables and fruits.

MONTH THREE

- 1 gallon of water per person and pets
- 2 bags of sprouting seeds
- 1 bag of garden seeds
- 1 large can dry fruit/vegetables.
- 1-pound nut or seeds (of choice)
- potting mix for garden and sprouting
- dry at least one tray of garden vegetables and fruits.

MONTH FOUR

- 1 gallon of water per person and pets
- sweetener (of choice)
- salt
- 1-pound grain (of choice)
- 1-pound garden seeds
- pet food,
- baby food, if needed
- dry at least one tray of garden vegetables and fruits.

MONTH FIVE

- 1 gallon of water per person and pets
- 1 bag of sprouting seeds
- 2 vegetables, dried or freeze-dried
- 1 fruit, dried or freeze-dried
- 1 homemade dried soup mixes per person
- 1-pound grain (of choice)
- dry at least one tray of garden vegetables and fruits.

MONTH SIX

- 1 gallon of water per person and pets
- dried fruit
- seasonings
- salt
- pet food,
- baby food, if needed
- dry at least one tray of garden vegetables and fruits.

MONTH SEVEN

- 1 gallon of water per person and pets
- 1 bag of sprouting seeds
- 1 bag of garden seeds
- 2 large cans of dried fruit/vegetables
- 1 homemade dried soup mixes per person
- box of dates
- dry at least one tray of garden vegetables and fruits.

MONTH EIGHT

- 1 gallon of water per person and pets
- 1 bag of sprouting seeds
- 2 large cans of dried fruit/vegetables
- 1-pound nuts/seeds
- dry lemons and limes for juice

MONTH NINE

- 1 gallon of water per person and pets
- 1 bag of sprouting seeds
- 2 large cans of dried fruit/vegetables
- 1-pound nuts/seeds
- pet food,
- baby food, if needed
- dry at least one tray of garden vegetables and fruits.

MONTH TEN

- 1 gallon of water per person and pets
- powdered greens
- garden seeds
- 1 gallon of water per person
- a good set of knives
- dry at least one tray of garden vegetables

MONTH ELEVEN

- 1 gallon of water per person and pets
- 1 bag of sprouting seeds
- 2 large cans of dried fruit/vegetables
- 1-pound nuts
- 1-pound seeds
- dried soup mix per person
- dry at least one tray of garden vegetables
- Disposable plates, cups and utensils (paper)

MONTH TWELVE

- 1 gallon of water per person and pets
- 1 bag sprouting seeds
- 5 gallons grains

- 1 can dry vegetables
- 1 can dried fruit

BONUS: Pet preparation

If you have a pet, it is essential to plan for their needs also. Some of the essentials to include are:

- minimum of three days' worth of food and water
- manual can opener
- extra medications
- leash, collar with ID
- pet carrier
- copies of veterinary records and registration
- recent photograph of the pet
- microchip information
- favorite toy/blanket

Chapter 5 How to Store

Food preservation is one of the oldest food preservation techniques used by humans. With time and innovation, many new and improved methods for food preservation have developed.

The basic concept behind food preservation is to slow down disease-causing bacteria activity and slow down the oxidation of fats that can cause rancidity.

The main methods are:
- Dehydration
- Freezing
- Freeze-Drying
- Fermentation
- Root Cellaring
- Gardening

Other conventional methods not covered in this book include:
- Canning
- Salting
- Smoking
- Vacuum sealing

DRYING

Foods dried at home under stable conditions produce a high-quality product. Compared with canning and freezing, which involve extreme temperatures. Food drying is the least damaging form of food preservation.

With the right combination of warmth, low humidity, and airflow, you can safely dry foods.

- Low humidity releases moisture from the food into the air.
- Low heat allows the warm temperature to evaporate moisture.
- Air circulation speeds up drying.

Organisms that spoil food require moisture to survive. Drying eliminates moisture from the food, resulting in longer shelf life. Foods that are completely dried have the most extended storage life.

Drying is the oldest method of preserving food. The first European settlers in America often ate dried corn, apples, currants, and grapes.

Produce picked in their prime have the best nutritional value. For the best quality product, choose only fresh, ripe unblemished foods to dry. Pre-treating minimizes oxidation. Dipping fruits into citrus juices (orange, lemon, or pineapple) helps retain colors.

Read ingredients to ensure that there are no preservatives or sugars added if purchasing dried food at the store. Do not buy any dried food with mold or an abnormal smell.

Whether food is home-dried or purchased, dried fruits and vegetables should be kept in an airtight container. Store in cooler, dry, and dark areas. The colder the area, the longer the shelf life and more nutritional value the food will have.

Soak dried food for at least 20 minutes before using it. When conserving water, add enough water to cover what you are rehydrating, plus 1 inch. Keep an eye on it and add more water if needed. When rehydrated, some dried food will not have the same texture as it did fresh (such as tomatoes).

Dried fruits and vegetables are high in fiber and carbohydrates and low in fat. However, dried foods are more calorically dense than their fresh counterparts. In recipes, the recommended serving size for dried fruits and vegetables is half that of fresh food.

The four most common methods for drying food used today are:

DEHYDRATOR:

This type of drying produces the highest quality product. Dehydrators dry food while retaining food quality uniformly. Most food dehydrators have an eclectic element for heat and a fan and vent for air circulation.

An electric dehydrator may be purchased, and various sizes and levels of quality are generally available. When deciding on a dehydrator, make sure it has a temperature control on it; otherwise, you are drying your food at about 225°F.

SOLAR:

Sun dryers generally have small capacity. Solar energy is an economical procedure, especially for smaller amounts, and requires 3 to 5 consecutive days of 95°F or above and low humidity.

If you live in an area with low relative humidity of less than 20% and direct sunlight, solar drying may be the right choice for you. If you don't have direct sun and higher humidity, the food will mold before it dries.

AIR DRYING:

Air Drying is similar to sun drying but takes place indoors in a well-ventilated room or screened-in porch. Unlike sun drying, air drying does depend on sunlight or enough heat from the sun, only low humidity below 60 percent is needed.

Herbs, hot peppers, and mushrooms are the most common air-dried items. They do not need any pretreating, just string them up, or tie into bundles and suspend until dry. A paper bag can be placed over them to protect from dust and other pollutants.

OVEN:

To dry food in a household kitchen, it can take around 5 to 6 hours, or more, to dry food properly, thicker or starchy foods may take longer. Oven-dried foods are often darker and more brittle than foods dried by other methods.

When using the oven for drying, use the warm setting on the lowest temperature. Higher than 140°F. and food will more likely cook instead of drying out. An oven thermometer will give an accurate reading of the drying temperature.

To improve air circulation when oven drying, crack the door open 2-4 inches and place a fan near the outside of the door.

FREEZING:

Freezing is the easiest and least time-consuming method of preserving foods. Freezing at 0°F inactivates microbes, bacteria, yeast, and mold, present in food. Once thawed, food starts to break down.

Freezing slows the movement of molecules, causing microbes to enter a dormant stage preserving food for extended periods (6 to 12 months). Quality suffers from lengthy freezer storage.

Freshness and quality at the time of freezing affect the condition of frozen foods. If frozen at peak harvest, foods emerge tasting better than foods frozen near the end of their useful life. The freezing process itself does not destroy nutrients, but they will break down over time.

Freeze food as fast as possible to maintain its quality. Rapid freezing prevents undesirable large ice crystals from forming throughout. Never stack packages to be frozen as they will not freeze properly. Stack them only after they have frozen solid.

To prevent freezer burn, remove all the air from the storage bag. One method is to use a straw. Place it a little opening and suck out all the air. For other containers, place plastic wrap right onto the surface to prevent contact with air and ice crystals. Always label and date your food to know when to rotate.

Generally, I recommend only freezing what you will use during the winter or within six months.

NOTE: Many people will blanch food before freezing. Blanching decreases 60 percent of the nutrients and destroys natural enzymes. I have successfully kept unbleached frozen food for six months before eating.

FREEZE-DRYING:

Photo by CC BY-SA 3.0

Freeze-drying or lyophilization is like "suspended animation" for food. It works by freezing food and then reducing the surrounding pressure and adding enough heat to allow the frozen water in the food to sublime (skip the liquid phase) and go directly from the solid phase to gas. The idea is to remove water while leaving the basic structure and composition of the food intact. The two significant factors that determine if a substance will be a solid, liquid, or gas are heat and atmospheric pressure.

Freeze-drying improves shelf life and reduces the total weight of the food. Research conducted by Sheffield Hallam University found that "freeze-drying strawberries resulted in zero loss of vitamin C...in contrast, fresh strawberries chilled for an equal time showed a vitamin C loss of 18%."

Freeze-dried food can be purchased or, if you have the money, buy a home freeze dryer.

FERMENTING:

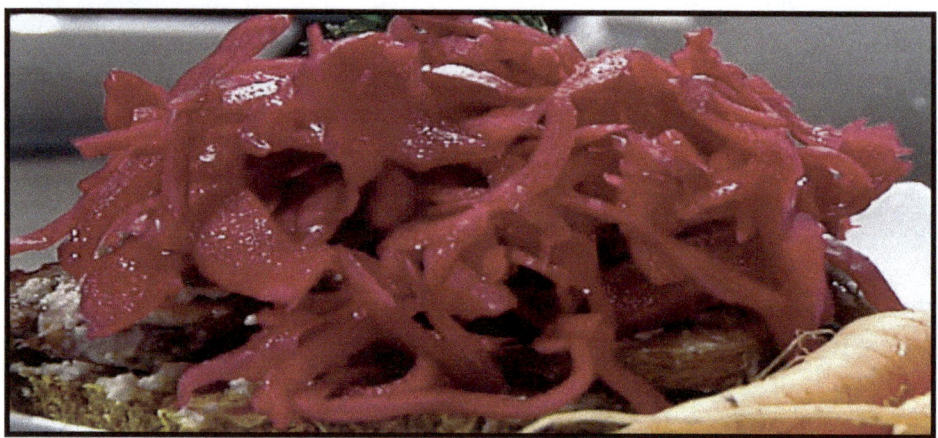

In general, fermentation is the chemical breakdown of a substance by bacteria, yeast, or other microorganisms in the absence of oxygen or anaerobic conditions.

During the fermentation process, microbes feed on sugars and starches, breaking down food. Fermentation can make conditions unsuitable for undesirable microorganisms, thus preserving food. Fermentation increases B and C vitamins, enhances folic acid, riboflavin, niacin, thiamin, and biotin. When the lactobacilli increase, the digestibility of vitamins and minerals is improved. Fermentation eliminates anti-nutrients, like phytic acid, which can cause mineral deficiencies.

Some examples of fermented foods include kimchi, kombucha, miso, and sauerkraut. Pickles and other soured (pickled) foods typically use brine, vinegar, or another acid such as lemon juice.

USING A ROOT CELLAR:

A root cellar has been a food storage preservation method for a long time. In the broadest sense, a root cellar is any form of storage that holds food in optimum conditions for an extended period by controlling the temperature, humidity, and light. They are an excellent way to maintain a food supply without electricity.

Root cellars are traditionally underground storage space. Some people have created a 'root cellar' in a garage, under a porch or any cool, dry place with a stable temperature (40-60°F).

Others dig a hole and bury old freezers then cover them--but one must be careful of children finding them and getting trapped. Using white sand in boxes or burlap bags is another way to preserve food in a root cellar style.

Foods that store well in a root cellar are typically hard, root vegetables --thus the name--such as carrots, squash, and turnips. And if done correctly, apples, pears, and sweet potatoes can be stored for many months. Winter squashes, including pumpkin store well.

To prepare root vegetables for winter storage, trim off green tops, leaving a one-inch stub. If left untrimmed the top growth will decay and encourage the deterioration of adjacent roots. Take care not to cut root flesh, and don't cut off root tips. It's better not to wash your vegetables, but gently brush off any large clumps of soil that may cling to them. Any skin break invites spoilage.

Cure certain vegetables to store them well. Expose garlic and onions to the sun for a week, and then spread them loosely in shallow boxes or hang them in net bags or old pantyhose for air circulation. Pumpkins and squash (except acorn squash) need to be cured in the sun for two weeks after harvesting to develop a hard rind. Always leave on the stems.

EXTENDING STORAGE LIFE:

The quality of the packaging is an essential success factor for food preservation. When storing food, you need to consider temperature, moisture, insects, and rodents. Be aware of possible risk of spoilage; when purchasing food look for the following signs:

- Integrity of the package--look for corrosion and dented cans.
- Bulging cans or packaging--bacterial or fungal growth can cause bulging.
- The appearance of food - if the food has anything on it that looks like mold or fungus--throw it out. And if there is a significant loss of color, it is an indication of reduced nutritional value.
- Odor versus aroma--if it has an odor of mildew or a putrid smell, discard it immediately. The food should smell pleasant. Strawberries should smell like strawberries. When in doubt, throw them out!

Moisture can become a problem with dried, freeze-dried foods, nuts, seeds, and grains. The most natural solution to keeping food dry is to store them in airtight containers.

Most importantly, be aware of the temperature where your food is stored. The recommendations of the USDA suggest; "every 5.6°C. (10.08°F) drop in temperature doubles the storage life of food."

Storage Life Differences Depending on Temperature	
Constant Storage Temp in °F	Storage Life in Years
39	40
49	30
59	20
70	10
80	5
90	2.5
100	1.25

NOTE: this chart is not for any specific food but indicates the relationship between temperature and storage life.

Even well packaged food stored in a warm environment will last a fraction of the time than if stored in a cool, dry place. Expect longer storage life if your storage temperature is at a constant 60°F or below. Frequent temperature changes shorten storage life.

Even if you don't have an ideal place, store food and improve its shelf life through a regular rotation cycle.

Chapter 6 Other Foods and Information

HONEY STORAGE:

Honey stores very well. Try to get raw honey from your local beekeepers, since it helps acclimate the body to your area, reduce allergies, and help build the immune system. Raw honey crystallizes over time. Incredibly, edible honey was found in tombs with Egyptian mummies!

Even though honey is edible after thousands of years, it is an excellent habit to rotate it. Comb honey doesn't store as well as liquid honey.

Storage containers should be opaque, airtight, moisture, and odor-proof. Storage temperature is not as crucial for honey, but keep it from freezing, and try not to expose honey to high temperatures. Storing honey in the refrigerator will cause it to crystallize quickly.

Exposure to air and moisture can cause its color to darken and flavor to intensify and may speed crystallization as well. If crystallization does occur, liquefy the honey by placing the container in hot water.

Avoid storing honey near heat sources. If using plastic pails, do not keep it near petroleum products (such as gasoline engines), chemicals, or any other odor-producing products. Protect your honey; it's an incredible food source and can be useful for healing salves.

OIL AND FAT STORAGE:

Fats are vital for the body and can make food taste satisfying, improving the taste of many dishes. The human body effectively uses healthy fats to absorb vitamins A, E, D, and K.

Fats and oils vary in their ability to store for prolonged periods. The problem is that they go rancid rather quickly. Rancid fats have been implicated in increased heart disease and other health risks, increasing the need for regular rotation.

Storing fats starts with proper food packaging. If possible, buy oils in opaque, airtight containers--preferably glass. Newly opened oil should be left in the original packaging or transferred carefully into a clean container. Even a small amount of old oil mixed with fresh oil will hasten rancidity. Vacuum sealing the oil in a storage container is one way to keep the oil fresh longer.

Generally, unopened oils last for about a year to a year and a half. Specialty oils, such as sesame or flaxseed oils, have a shorter shelf life. Once opened, oils can begin to go rancid in a week to a few months. It may not smell bad until several months after opening.

Temperature can also dramatically affect the storage life and quality of fats and oils. All fats and foods containing fat keep better in colder storage areas. Reducing exposure to humidity, air, light, and warm temperatures will prolong storage life.

DRYING NUTS AND SEEDS:

To store nuts and seeds, make sure they are dry. For foraged nuts, treat them for bugs or eggs. You can do this by removing the husk from the nuts and allow them to dry completely. Then, once the nuts are dry, freeze them for 48 hours. Then they can be stored like commercially produced nuts.

If you are buying nuts and seeds from a store, think about skipping the bulk bins. You have no idea how long they've been out in open air. Oxygen is the number one enemy for a nut's shelf life.

Storing nuts and seeds in an airtight container can keep them dry, in or out of the shell. Nuts in shells keep longer; however, shelled nuts are more convenient, and I like to store both.

By labeling nuts and seeds with the date of storage, rotation becomes easy. Store them in a cupboard for three months, a refrigerator for up to six months, or freeze them for over a year.

SALT:

Salt is not a spice, but a mineral and doesn't typically lose flavor over time like spices and herbs. There are two types of edible salts; sea salt and mined salt. There are enormous differences between refined table salt and natural salts, which can have a significant impact on health. If you want your body to function correctly, you need unrefined salt, complete with all-natural elements.

89% of all sea salt producers now refine their salt, and "sea salt" is not as healthy as it used to be as the oceans have become dumping grounds for harmful toxic poisons.

Look for an unrefined salt to store. I prefer pure mineral-rich Himalayan Crystal Salt. Just be aware, like sea salt, many companies now refine Himalayan salt.

The Fresenius Institute in Europe analyzed Himalayan Crystal Salt and discovered it carries an array of essential trace minerals and elements, such as; potassium, calcium, magnesium, and so forth. Minerals help the body achieve balance. Himalayan salt can help restore fluids and replenish the body's electrolytes after sweating.

The following information comes from Healthline.com ;

Well-known minerals found in a gram	Pink Himalayan Salt	Table Salt
Calcium (mg)	1.6	0.4
Potassium (mg)	2.8	0.9
Magnesium (mg)	1.06	0.0139
Iron (mg)	0.0369	0.0101
Sodium	368	381

SPICES:

Long-term food storage does not have to be boring and bland. Eating good tasting food and enjoying your food promotes a healthier mindset. One of the ways to make food taste delicious is to pay attention to the spices you use.

Ground spices and herbs have a storage life of 2-3 years. Dried whole spices and herbs have a storage life 3-5 years if properly stored. To preserve the best flavor, store spices and herbs in a cool, dry place, away from exposure to bright light, heat, moisture or oxygen. Storing herbs and spices in the refrigerator isn't ideal since the humid environment can alter the flavor.

Herbs are the leafy green parts of plants. Herbals can be single herbs or combinations to be used for medicinal uses also. Some common culinary herbs include sage, oregano, parsley, thyme, basil, chives, rosemary, and mint.

Spices refer to the root, stem, bulb, bark, or seeds of a plant. Some common culinary spices include cinnamon, ginger, cloves, nutmeg, vanilla, and cumin.

SPICE COMBINATIONS:

Barbecue Seasoning: salt, sugar, garlic, hot red pepper, hickory, and onion

Cajun Seasoning: onion, chilies, salt, with white, black, and red peppers.

Chili Seasoning: chili powder, cumin, oregano, coriander, garlic, allspice, and cloves

Five-Spice: cinnamon, star anise (or anise seed), fennel seeds, black pepper, cloves

Italian Seasoning: oregano, marjoram, thyme, rosemary, basil, and sage

Mediterranean Seasoning: basil, oregano, salt, parsley, onion, black pepper

Mexican Seasoning: cumin, chili pepper, salt, onion, sweet peppers, garlic, oregano, and red pepper

Pizza Seasoning: onion, fennel, oregano, basil, garlic, bell peppers, chilies, marjoram, parsley, and thyme

Poultry Seasoning: sage, thyme, onion, marjoram, black pepper, celery seed, and red pepper

Pumpkin Pie Spice: cinnamon, nutmeg, cloves, and ginger

Ranch Seasoning: parsley, dill, garlic, onion, black pepper, salt

Salt-Free Seasoning: garlic, onion, chili, paprika, parsley, black pepper

Zip Spice: onion, paprika, chili pepper, cumin, garlic, jalapeno, coriander, cayenne, oregano, and lemon oil

Store the spices needed to make the blends, or pre-make them and label the container as such

Chapter 7 Gardening

GARDENING:

A garden can be anywhere and grow anything you choose. There is no set size or location for a garden, whether it is an herb, indoor, container, or traditional yard garden. There is a satisfaction knowing that there is fresh food coming up and renewing your food supply.

Think about how much time and space you have before growing a garden. Perhaps start with growing herbs or vegetables in pots to experience the satisfaction of a small fresh supply of organic food.

LONG TERM SEED STORAGE:

All viable seeds are tiny hibernating plants that only need moisture and warmth to sprout. Contained in seeds are the nutrients it needs to spring into existence. Seeds need to be kept cool and dry, and if the time came where food was in short supply or became too expensive, stored seeds could be a lifeline.

Storing seeds are similar to storing food. The enemy to seeds are heat, light, and humidity. Keep seeds fresh by avoiding fluctuations in temperature, and light, store them in moisture-proof containers. You can keep seeds in a jar with a tightfitting lid in the refrigerator or a cool, dark place. It is a good idea to rotate seeds every few years. To keep the moisture out, use a moisture absorber, such as a silica gel packet. Two scoops of rice can be added in with larger seeds to absorb the moisture.

Cucumbers from my indoor garden

NOTE: silica gel, made from silicon, is sourced from the crust of the earth and, with its porous oxygen atoms, readily absorbs moisture.

Seeds for sprouting and growing can last in the refrigerator for nearly three years. Be sure to write the date you store the seeds on the container. Remember to allow seeds to come to room temperature before planting.

To harvest seeds, spread them out to prevent them from sticking together and be allowed to air dry. Then place the seeds in labeled envelopes before storing.

After long-term storage, test their germination ability by taking ten seeds and placing them in a plastic bag, adding a wet folded dampened paper towel. Then put it in a warm place on the counter, making sure the air can flow through. If 9 out of 10 seeds sprout, then the germination rate is 90%. Look for non-GMO seeds (not genetically modified) and non-hybrid seeds to grow and cultivate seeds for many years.

INDOOR GARDEN:

Many live in places where they think they cannot "grow a garden," such as in apartments or condominium communities. You don't need a huge yard to have a productive garden. Many people have grown vegetables in pots, and yes, they can be successfully grown indoors-- look at my bell pepper photo.

Red bell pepper grown indoors

An indoor garden can take as much or little space as you have. First, assess the amount of space you have available. While you may not have much room space, try thinking up and use vertical shelves and tables. Almost anything can be grown indoors if it does not become too large by nature. Try a "permaculture" technique and grow plants with similar watering and lighting needs together. Then create a watering and plant care schedule, such as every Friday, care for plants.

I have consistently grown tomatoes, bell peppers, and cucumbers inside our small apartment. Some indoor plants that do well include lettuce, microgreens, mustard greens, radishes, scallions, and most herbs such as basil, parsley, oregano, chives, rosemary, etc. Pick your favorites and grow them! I also like to grow marigolds and other pretty flowers for insect control--and pure joy.

WHAT YOU WILL NEED:

Pots or Growing Containers: If you are using a 5-gallon bucket, then drill holes in the bottom for water to drain. If I am growing indoors, I like to use fabric bags. Inclement weather, late blight, and critter problems can cause vegetable failure when growing in pots outside on a patio.

Water Saucer: Water can spill or overflow. It is a good idea to have something to collect water and keep from getting floors wet.

Seeds and Plants: I have learned to grow my garden from seeds. The plants I bought from the store tend to carry other insects (spider mites, aphids) that hurt my plants that are growing well.

TIP: Buy seeds designed to grow in containers or pots. They usually work better and are not as tall.

Lighting: Direct or indirect lighting, natural or grow lights for winter months. The plants need sunlight, but if it is too hot, they can burn and die off. Find a place where your garden gets light and is moderate in temperature, without drafts of heat or cold. If desired, you can buy a grow light. There are several types to choose from; incandescent, fluorescent, compact fluorescent, and high-intensity discharge.

Good soil: Outside soil is not the best choice. It tends to be compact or dense and may contain weed seeds and insect pests. Use a high-quality mix for vegetables with a complete fertilizer or add it in later to the potting soil. An excellent growing media should remain loose and drain well and still contain enough organic matter to hold nutrients and moisture.

Vegetable food/fertilizer: Feed your plants slow-releasing fertilizer or those specific to their growth. Talk with the gardener

Dwarf Tiny Tim tomatoes from my indoor garden

in your supply store for the ideal nutrients, or look it up online. Supplement the plant food weekly or as directed by the manufacturer.

Growing Plants: Start by growing seeds in a small pot until it grows into a small plant. Once the plant has grown large enough, transplant it to the prepared container. Plant your seedling deep in the soil so it can grow strong roots.

Watering: Be consistent in your watering schedule, and be careful not to overwater them! Inconsistent watering--either too much and then too little-- can cause vegetables to crack and split. Water the soil, not the leaves. Wet leaves can encourage fungus to grow. Harvest your "garden" when the food is ripe. You will reap the rewards for your efforts, knowing that you raised them with care, and you now will enjoy them when they are at their highest nutritional content --with the benefit of tasting better right off the plant! Children benefit by learning how to grow vegetables and herbs and develop a desire for natural foods.

NOTE: a lack of humidity in the home can be a problem for vegetables. Seeing the tips of leaves turning brown, plants looking withered or puckered, plants losing their leaves are signs that humidity needs to increase. Some ways to improve the humidity in the room is to mist plants daily or to place a tray filled with rocks and water near the garden for natural evaporation. Another method is to place plants close together to create a supportive "micro-environment", or lastly, run an electric humidifier.

SPROUTING:

When a seed germinates and begins to sprout, energy is released, and natural chemical changes occur, making it easier for the human body to assimilate the available nutrients.

Seeds, nuts, grains, and beans contain enzyme inhibitors that keep the seeds from growing. Nature protects seeds with this inhibitor until they become germinated. Cooking destroys these enzyme inhibitors, but it also destroys enzymes. Sprouting is a simple way to get rid of the enzyme inhibitors while preserving life-giving enzymes.

There are many methods of sprouting (jar, paper-towel, tray, etc.). All sprouting starts with water by soaking the seeds overnight, then placing them in a container to protect them while they sprout, such as a large glass jar or a flat tray. After soaking them overnight, pour fresh water into the sprouting jar, with the seeds, and then rinse it with a mesh cover to keep the sprouts from coming out of the sprouting jar when rinsing. Gently shake the seeds back to the sides of the jar to give them room to grow. Or, if using a flat tray, lightly spritz the seeds/sprouts with water. Water sprouting seeds two times a day. Make sure the water drains completely. Sprouts are ready when they start growing tails (1 to 6 days). If you rinse and drain the sprouts every three days after harvesting and store them in the refrigerator, they keep up to a week.

NOTE: Some bean sprouts, such as pinto beans, are bitter and best not eaten raw.

NOTE: Sprouts from the nightshade family (tomatoes, peppers, eggplant, potatoes) should not be eaten as they are toxic.

Sprouted or bloomed black wild rice.

Sprouting Rice: When rice sprouts, it is called blooming. Start by soaking the rice in water, changing the water every day.

Soak 1-2 cups of rice in half a gallon of water overnight. Drain and rinse it, then add fresh water. Rinse the rice every day, keeping it covered in water for about three days (the length of sprouting time may vary based on climate).

The rice is ready to eat when it is soft and comfortable to chew. Some wild black rice will split down the middle, and look like it is blooming outward, but it is not considered a sprout. Some people "bloom" rice by placing the rice in a food processor to score the seed coat, and then soak it in pure water as described above. Brown rice will sprout but does not taste very good-- in my opinion. (White rice will not germinate).

> **TIP:** When sprouting rice, 1 cup of dry rice equals 2 cups sprouted.
>
> **NOTE:** "Wild rice" is not rice but an aquatic grass native to North America and is ready to eat after soaking for 2-3 days.
>
> **NOTE:** Quinoa is bloomed the same way as rice, but there is no need to score it because the seeds are so small.

Chapter 8 Kitchen Equipment

When you are planning equipment for food storage, it is essential to determine if it will work without power and how much water it takes to clean.

Electricity may not always be available in times when living off food storage. I like looking at camping stores and talking to people who don't use all the various gadgets--but live simple like the Amish.

The following is a list of equipment you may want to purchase;

Sprouting equipment: I like trays. Use whatever method you enjoy and with which you have the most success. Keep in mind the water needed for future sprouting needs--and possible emergencies.

Spiral slicer: is for vegetable noodles. Or, if you don't have one, shred the vegetables using a cheese grater or mandolin.

Dehydrator: When looking for a dehydrator, look into solar-powered or air-drying ones. I have found a few by searching the Internet.

Food Processor: Look for hand-operated processors, although they do not mix as nicely as electric ones.

Blenders: There are bicycle blenders where you pedal a stationary bike to make the blender work. (These blenders seem to work very well.)

I have seen a few kinds of non-electric blenders, such as hand-operated ones, where you turn the crank. (I have not been very impressed with these as they are not very powerful). Look online to see if there are any Amish-type blenders and kitchen tools since they use no electricity as a rule.

Rechargeable camping blenders are another option, although if the power is out, you will need a way to recharge.

Other Very Useful Items: A good set of knives, cutting board, bowls, and pans.

Nonstick Dehydrator Sheets: keep food from sticking to dehydrator. Unbleached parchment paper can also be used.

Generator: When choosing a generator, make sure it will suit your needs. Will it have enough power to do what you want? How hard is it to start? What kind of fuel does it use? Will you be able to store that fuel safely? Does it have multiple outlets? Is it for indoor use or outdoors? How big is it? Can it be moved easily?

Never use generators indoors unless the manufacturer says it is safe to do so!

Solar energy charging station: These units can be expensive, but well worth it if you think you will not have electricity or fuel for a while. If there is time to save up for it, and direct sunlight where you live, these can be well worth it.

Other Items: A good set of knives, cutting board, bowls, pans, hand-operated can opener, camping style water filter, portable water filter, and water bottle. A thermos to put hot water in with soaked grains or your favorite breakfast mix for a nice warm meal on the go.

Chapter 9 Menu Ideas

Using and practicing recipes before stressful times will help calm the body and ease the stress when difficult times come, and with preparation ahead of time, bring invaluable peace of mind.

Be sure to select menus that you think your family may like --and test them out now! Start by planning two-week menus. Once you decide which recipe and menu you or your family enjoys, then multiplying them by six, now you will have an assorted three-month idea of what food to store and supply. Again, as you test the recipes, pick your favorites, list the ingredients, put them on your grocery list, and then start to store them for your food supply.

Keep adding to your supplies following the recipes you like. Make another two weeks' worth of menus and multiply them by six for a six-month supply for food storage. Keep this up until you have an enjoyable, well-rounded one-year food supply.

If you are having trouble with menu planning, try thinking about themes instead; for example, plan a Juice Day, a Soup Day, an Italian Day, Mexican Day, Pizza Day, Birthday, and so forth. Involve your family and have fun with this!

Food Storage Dinner--Bean Burrito (page 91) made with sunflower Beans (page 91) and Mexi-Rice, (page 87) Almond Sour Cream (page 105) and Sprouts

TIP: Update your menus regularly to meet your family's changing needs, i.e., new members, new favorite recipes, seasons, and dietary changes.

The following is four days of a sample menu. The second set of forms are a week of blank forms to fill in your list.

TIP: Make copies of the forms and use them as needed. To learn how much you need to store, you need to know just how much food the recipe makes, so if the recipe says it makes four servings--and you have a family of four--times that amount by six for a three-months supply, and so forth. If the recipe makes two servings, and you have four people to feed, double the recipe. Then multiply that by six for your three months' supply.

Food Storage Celebration Cake (page 124)

Sunday

Recipe Location	Ingredients	Amount Needed for 6 Months
	2 c. walnuts	12 c.
Breakfast	2 c. oat groats, flaked	12 c.
	1 c. coconut sugar	6 c.
	1 c. dates	6 c.
Yummy Oatmeal	½ c. almond butter	3 c.
Cookies	1 tsp. Himalayan crystal salt	6 tsp.
(Thriving page 132)	2 tsp. coconut oil	12 tsp.
	1 tsp. turmeric	6 tsp.
	-----	-----
Nut Milk	1 c. Almonds	6 c.
(Thriving page 71)	2 c. Pure Water	12 c.
	-----	-----
	1 c. Almonds,	6 c. ,
Lunch	1 c. Lemon Juice	6 c.
	¼ c. Cold Pressed Olive Oil	1 ½ c.
Herbed Almond	1 tbsp. Garlic Powder	6 tbsp.
	¼ tsp. Himalayan Crystal Salt	1 ½ tsp.
Spread	1 tsp. Mustard Powder	6 tsp.
(Thriving page 97)	¼ c. Dried Parsley	1 ½ c.
	¼ c. Water	1 ½ c.
	-----	-----
Crackers	1 c. flax seeds	6 c.
(Thriving page 108)	¾ c. water	4 ½ c.
	¼ tsp. Himalayan crystal salt	1 ½ tsp.
	-----	-----
Sprouts	1 c. golden flax seed	6 c.
	1 c. buckwheat	6 c.
Dinner	1 tbsp. Himalayan crystal salt	6 tbsp.
	1-2 c. pure water	12 c.
	¼ c. raw coconut flour	1 ½ c.
Olive Pizza	½ c. sun dried olives	3 c.
(Thriving page 95)	½ c. artichokes hearts	3 c.
	1 c. nut mayo	6c.
	1 c. dried tomatoes	6 c.
Sprout Salad	1 tbsp. pizza seasoning	6 tbsp.
(Thriving page 77)	2 tbsp. olive oil	12 tbsp.
	1 tbsp. lemon juice	6 tbsp.
	-----	-----
with Italian	1 c. mung bean spouts	6 c.
Dressing	1 c. mixed microgreens	6 c.
(Thriving page 75)	1 c. tender green	6 c.
	-----	-----
	3 tbsp. cold pressed olive oil	18 tbsp.
	1 tsp. raw apple cider vinegar	6 tsp.
	½ tsp. dried parsley	3 tsp.
	4 tbsp. lemon juice	24 tbsp.
	½ tsp. garlic powder	3 tsp.
	½ tsp. dried basil	3 tsp.
	¼ tsp. crushed red pepper	3 tsp.
	½ tsp. dried oregano	3 tsp.

Monday

Recipe Location	Ingredients	Amount Needed for 6 Months
Breakfast Iron Passion (Thriving page 55) Lemon Poppy Seed Muffins (Thriving page 112) **Lunch** Kamut Salad with Vinaigrette (Thriving page 79) **Dinner** Wild Rice and Microgreen Salad (Thriving page 82) Carob 'Ice Cream' (Thriving page 119)	• ¼ c. apricots • 1 tbsp. pumpkin seeds • 4 carrots • ¼ c. spinach • ½ lemon, juiced • 2 tsp. kelp powder • 2 c. coconut water ----- • 1 c. cashews • 1 c. almond pulp • 1 lemon, juiced • 1 c. dates • 1 tbsp. lemon zest (peel) • 1 tbsp. poppy seeds • 1 tsp. Himalayan Crystal Salt ----- • 1 c. kamut or wheat berries • ¾ c. dried red bell pepper • ¾ c. dried yellow bell pepper • ¾ c. dried small summer squash • ¾ c. dried tomatoes, chopped • 3 tbsp. cold pressed olive oil • 3 tbsp. raw apple cider vinegar • 2 tbsp. onion powder • 1 tbsp. water • 1 tbsp. mustard powder • 1 tbsp. garlic powder • 1 tsp. cayenne pepper • 1 tsp. thyme • ½ tsp. Himalayan crystal salt • black pepper to taste ----- • ¾ c. wild rice, sprouted • 2 tbsp. dried flat leaf parsley • 2 tbsp. dried or fresh mint leafs • 2 tbsp. dried or fresh dill • ½ c. microgreen sprouts • ¼ c. almonds, chopped • ½ tsp. onion powder • Himalayan crystal salt • pepper to taste • 2 tbsp. lemon juice • 2 tbsp. cold pressed olive oil ----- • 1 c. cashews • 1 ½ c. water • ¼ c. dried stevia leaves • 1 tsp. Himalayan crystal salt • ½ c. carob powder	1½ c. 6 tbsp. 24 1½ c. 3 12 tsp. 12 c. ----- 6 c. 6 c. 6 6 c. 6 tbsp. 6 tbsp. 6 tsp. ----- 6 c. 4½ c. 4½ c. 4½ c. 4½ c. 18 tbsp. 18 tbsp. 12 tbsp. 6 tbsp. 6 tbsp. 6 tbsp. 6 tsp. 6 tsp. 3 tsp. to taste ----- 4½ c. 12 tbsp. 12 tbsp. 12 tbsp. 3 c. 1½ c. 3 tsp. to taste to taste 12 tbsp. 12 tbsp. ----- 6 c. 9 c. 1½ c. 6 tsp. 3 c.

Tuesday (Holiday Plan)

Recipe Location	Ingredients	Amount Needed for 6 Months
Breakfast Nut Yogurt with Rehydrated Fruit (Thriving page 100)	• 1 c. macadamia nuts or cashews • 1 c. almond pulp • 1 tsp. vanilla • 2 c. rejuvelac • ½ dried fruit of choice	6 c. 6 c. 6 tsp. 12 c. 3
Lunch Sprouted Soup (Thriving page 83) Bread Sticks (Thriving page 115) **Dinner** Stuffing (Thriving page 96)	----- • 1-2 c. mixed bean and grain spouts • ½ c. dried carrot • ½ c. dried celery • ¼ c. dried onion • 2 tbsp. garlic powder • 1 c. dried red bell pepper • ¾ c. dried tomatoes, chopped • Himalayan crystal salt • 2 ½ tsp. poultry seasoning • 1 c. microgreen sprouts ----- • 1 c. gold flax • 3 c. buckwheat • 2 tsp. Himalayan crystal salt • ¼ c. raw coconut flour ----- • 2 c. dried celery • ½ c. dried onion • ½ c. dried apple • ¼ c. dried celery slices • ¼ c. dried carrot • ¼ c. raisins • 1 c. pecans, soaked • 1 c. almonds, soaked • ½ c. golden flax seeds • 2 tbsp. cold pressed olive oil • ¼ tsp. cayenne pepper • ½ tsp. garlic powder • ½ tsp. turmeric powder • 1 tsp. Himalayan crystal salt • pepper to taste -continued on next page	----- 6-12 c. 3 c. 3 c. 1½ c. 12 tbsp. 6 c. 4½ c. to taste 15 tsp. 6 c. ----- 6 c. 18 c. 12 tsp. 1½ c. ----- 12 c. 3 c. 3 c. 1½ c. 1½ c. 1½ c. 6 c. 6 c. 3 c. 12 tbsp. 1½ tsp. 3 tsp. 1½ tsp. 6 tsp. to taste

Tuesday Continued

Recipe Location	Ingredients	Amount Needed for 6 Months
Dinner continued Microgreen Salad (Thriving page 78) Fiesta Dressing (Thriving page 74) Apple Pie (Thriving page 139)	-continued • 1 c. microgreens • ¼ c. walnuts • ½ c. parsley from herb garden • 4 tbsp. rawmesan • ½ c. sunflower greens • 1 c. tender greens • Himalayan crystal salt to taste • black pepper to taste ----- • 4 tbsp. cold pressed olive oil • 2 tbsp. raw apple cider vinegar • 1 tsp. onion powder • ½ c. dried lime juice • Himalayan crystal salt • white pepper to taste ----- • 1 ½ c. pecans • ½ c. dates • 6 c. apples • ¼ lemon, juiced • 1 tsp. nutmeg • ½ tsp. cloves • 1 tbsp. vanilla extract • ¼ tsp. cold pressed olive oil • ¼ tsp. turmeric • ¼ tsp. Himalayan crystal salt • ¼ c. raw coconut sugar • ¼ c. raw almond butter • 1 ½ c. macadamia nuts or cashews • 1 ½ c. coconut, shredded	 6 c. 1½ c. 3 c. 24 tbsp. 3 c. 6 c. to taste to taste ----- 24 tbsp. 12 tbsp. 6 tsp. 3 c. to taste to taste ----- 9 c. 3 c. 36 c. 1½ 6 tsp. 3 tsp. 6 tbsp. 1½ tsp. 1½ tsp. 1½ tsp. 1½ c. 1½ c. 9 c. 9 c

Wednesday

Recipe Location	Ingredients	Amount Needed for 6 Months
Breakfast Raw Bagels (Thriving page 118) Herbed Cream Cheese (Thriving page 104) **Lunch** Taco Soup with Sprouts (Thriving page 99) Veggie Crackers (Thriving page 110)	• 1 c. buckwheat • ½ c. raw coconut four • ½ c. flaxseeds • 1 c. walnuts • 2 tbsp. chia seeds • 1 clove garlic • 2 tbsp. onion • 2 tbsp. coconut nectar • 1 lemon, juiced • 1 c. water • ¼ c. cashews ----- • ½ c. cashews • ½ c. pumpkin seeds • 2 lemons, juiced • ½ tsp. Himalayan crystal salt • ½ tsp. fresh or dried chives • ½ tsp. dried oregano • ½ tsp. dried parsley • ½ tsp. dried basil • ¼ tsp. dried dill ----- • 2 c. adzuki beans • ¼ c. tomatoes • ½ c. dried onion • 1 c. dried zucchini • 1 garlic clove • Mexican spice to taste • chili powder to taste • Himalayan crystal salt • pepper to taste • 2 c. dried corn • ½ tbsp. dried mushrooms ----- • 1 cloves garlic • ½ c. tomato • 1 c. carrots • 1 c. raw sunflower seeds • 1 c. raw pumpkin seeds • ½ c. dried red bell pepper • ½ c. dried onion • ½ c. dried celery stalks • 1 tsp. caraway seeds • 1 tsp. Himalayan crystal salt • 2 tbsp. cold pressed olive oil • 3 tbsp. raw tahini -continued on next page	6 c. 3 c. 3 c. 6 c. 12 tbsp. 6 12 tbsp. 12 tbsp. 6 6 c. 1½ c. ----- 3 c. 3 c. 12 3 tsp. 3 tsp. 3 tsp. 3 tsp. 3 tsp. 1½ tsp. ----- 2 c. 1½ c. 3 c. 6 c. 6 to taste to taste to taste to taste 12 c. 3 tbsp. ----- 6 3 c. 6 c. 6 c. 6 c. 3 c. 3 c. 3 c. 6 tsp. 6 tsp. 12 tbsp. 18 tbsp.

Wednesday Continued

Recipe Location	Ingredients	Amount Needed for 6 Months
Dinner Bean Burrito (Thriving page 91) Mexi-Rice (Thriving page 87) Almond Sour Cream (Thriving page 105) Sprouts	-continued • 1 ½ c. dried tomatoes • 1 tsp. garlic powder • 2 tsp. Himalayan crystal salt • ½ c. flax • 1 tbsp. onion powder • 1 small dried hot pepper • 2½ c. sunflower seeds • ¼ c. cold pressed olive oil • 3 ½ tsp. onion powder • 1 tbsp. chili powder • 2 tsp. cumin seed powder • 1 tsp. Himalayan crystal salt • 1 tbsp. raw apple cider vinegar • ½ c. dried bell pepper • sprouts ----- • 2 c. organic wild rice • ¼ c. onion, chopped • 1 c. dried red bell pepper • 3 tbsp. dried hot pepper • ¾ c. tomatoes • 2 tbsp. chili powder • 2 tsp. Himalayan crystal salt • 1 tsp. turmeric ----- • 1 c. almonds • 1 tsp. lemon juice powder • 1 tbsp. raw apple cider vinegar • ½ c. pure water as needed • Himalayan crystal salt	 3 c. 6 tsp. 12 tsp. 3 c. 12 tbsp. 6 15 c. 1½ c. 21 tsp. 6 tbsp. 12 tsp. 6 tsp. 6 tbsp. 3 c. 18 c. 3 c ----- 12 c. 3 c. 6 c. 18 tbsp. 4½ c. 12 tbsp. 12 tsp. 6 tsp. ----- 6 c. 6 tsp. 6 tbsp. 3 c. to taste

Sunday

Recipe Location	Ingredients	Amount Needed for 6 Months

Monday

Recipe Location	Ingredients	Amount Needed for 6 Months

Tuesday

Recipe Location	Ingredients	Amount Needed for 6 Months

Recipe Location	Ingredients	Amount Needed for 6 Months

Wednesday

Thursday

Recipe Location	Ingredients	Amount Needed for 6 Months

Friday

Recipe Location	Ingredients	Amount Needed for 6 Months

Saturday

Recipe Location	Ingredients	Amount Needed for 6 Months

Chapter 10
Just Add Water Recipes

Break out of the old food storage rut by making the following recipes beforehand. When you need them, all you need to do is add water before serving.

TIP: When you make soup, double it and then dry half of it for your storage. Then on long days or days when you don't want to prepare food, use the dry soup-- replace it when you make soup the next time. Easy!

1. Double your soup recipe, and dehydrate half of the soup.
2. Powder the dried soup and then simply rehydrate the soup with water!

make soup

dry soup

powder soup

rehydrate soup

Happy Juice

Makes 2-4 Servings

Ingredients

- 1 c. arugula
- 3-7 carrots
- ¼ beet
- ½ inch ginger root
- 1 lemon
- 1 apple

Directions

Run arugula, carrots, beat, ginger, lemon, and apple through a juicer or a blender.

Place the drink on a nonstick dehydrator sheet and dry.

Once the Happy Juice is dehydrated, break off pieces and powder it either in a food processor or coffee grinder. Pour the powder into a bag and label it with the packaging date.

To DRINK: Add about 2-4 cups of water and let sit for about 20 minutes. Stir it to make sure it is well mixed. Add water to taste.

Iron Passion

Makes 2-4 Servings

Ingredients

- ¼ c. apricots
- 1 tbsp. pumpkin seeds
- 4 carrots
- ¼ c. spinach
- ½ lemon, juiced
- 2 tsp. kelp powder
- ½ c. coconut water

Directions

Blend spinach, apricots, carrots, and lemon, and pumpkin seeds, kelp with coconut water. Blend until very smooth.

Pour onto dehydrator sheets and start the drying process. Halfway through, flip and remove the nonstick sheet and continue drying.

Once the drink is dried, break off pieces and powder it in either in a food processor or coffee grinder. Place the powder in a bag and label it.

To DRINK: Add about 2-4 cups of water and let sit for about 20 minutes. Stir it to make sure it is well mixed. Add water to taste.

Fun Fact

Dried veggies lose very little of their nutritional value when they go thru the dehydration process. They retain most of the minerals, most of the vitamin A and some of the B-vitamins. What they lose are the volatile nutrients like Vitamin C and beta carotene you can minimize this loss by dehydrating at lower temperatures.

Peach Mint Lemonade

Makes 2-4 Servings

Ingredients

- 4 fresh peaches
- 2 medium lemons
- 3 medium apples
- ½ c. raw liquid sweetener (optional)
- 2 tbsp. fresh mint
- ½ c. pure water

Directions

Juice arugula, carrots; peel the peaches, lemons mint, and apples.

If you don't have a juicer use a blender. Strain mixture into a bowl though a cheesecloth.

Pour onto dehydrator sheets and start the drying process. Halfway through, flip and remove the nonstick sheet and continue to dry.

Once the drink is dried, break off pieces and powder it in either in a food processor or coffee grinder. Place the powder in a bag and label it.

To DRINK: Add about 2-4 cups of water and let sit for about 20 minutes. Stir it to make sure it is well mixed. Add water to taste.

Tropical Smoothie

Makes 2-4 Servings

Ingredients

- ½ c. coconut water
- 1 c. mango, cubed
- 2 bananas
- 1 c. pineapple, chunks
- ½ lime, juiced

Directions

In a blender, combine coconut water, mango, bananas, pineapple, and lime juice. Blend until smooth.

Pour the juice on a nonstick dehydrator sheet and dry.

Halfway through, flip it, and remove the nonstick sheet, continue to dry.

Once drink is dehydrated, break off pieces and powder it either in a food processor or coffee grinder. Pour powder into a bag and label it.

To DRINK: Add about 2-4 cups of water and let it sit for about 20 minutes. Stir it to make sure it is well mixed. Start with less water, and add more as desired.

Watermelon Strawberry Drink

Makes 2-4 Servings

Ingredients

- 2 c. strawberries
- 2 c. watermelon
- 1 tbsp. fresh or dried stevia
- ½ c. water
- fresh mint, for garnish (optional)

Directions

Puree strawberries, watermelon, and stevia until smooth.

Place the drink on a nonstick dehydrator sheet, Halfway through the drying process, flip it over onto the rack and remove the nonstick sheet. Dehydrate completely.

Break off pieces and powder it in a food processor or coffee grinder. Place the powder in a bag and label it.

To DRINK: Add about 2-4 cups of water and let sit for about 20 minutes. Stir it to make sure it is well mixed. Start with less water, and add more as needed. Garnish with fresh mint and serve.

Garden Soup

Makes 4-6 Servings

Ingredients

- ¼ c. green onions, chopped
- 1 c. mung beans, sprouted
- ½ c. kale, sprouted
- ½ c. turnip, diced
- ½ c. carrots, sliced
- ½ c. celery, sliced
- ½ c. zucchini, chopped
- ½ c. summer yellow squash, chopped
- ½ c. cabbage, shredded
- 2 c. tomatoes soaked
- ½ tsp. Himalayan crystal salt
- ½ tsp. black pepper
- ½ tsp. basil, dried
- ½ tsp. oregano, dried
- ½ tsp. rosemary, dried
- ½ tsp. garlic powder

Directions

AHEAD OF TIME: Chop and prepare green onions, turnips, carrots, celery, zucchini, yellow squash, cabbage, and tomatoes and dry them. Store them in a bag with dried basil, oregano, rosemary, garlic powder, and salt.

In separate bags, place mung beans and kale seeds.

To EAT: Sprout mung beans and kale seeds **AHEAD OF TIME.**

Soak dried vegetables in about 4 cups of water and set aside. Mix the spices in with vegetables and top with the sprouts.

May warm to 100° F. Test with your finger.

Broccoli Soup

Makes 4-6 Servings

Ingredients

- ½ c. coconut water
- 1 c. mango, cubed
- 2 bananas
- 1 c. pineapple, chunks
- ½ lime, juiced

Directions

In a blender, purée cashews, onion, garlic, olive oil, broccoli, parsley, and lemon juice --add water as needed-- blend until smooth.

Place soup on a nonstick dehydrator sheet and dry. Flipping and removing the nonstick sheet halfway through.

Once soup is completely dry. Break off pieces and powder it either in food processor or coffee grinder. Place the powder in a bag and label.

For floaters in the soup dry broccoli flowerets and place in the bag with powdered soup.

To EAT: add about 2-4 cups of water and let sit for about 20 minutes. Stir it to make sure it is well mixed. Start with less water and add more water as desired.

Taco Soup

Makes 4-6 Servings

Ingredients

- 2 c. adzuki beans, sprouted
- 1 ½ c. corn
- ¼ c. tomatoes
- ½ c. onion, chopped
- 1 c. zucchini, chopped
- 1 garlic clove
- ½ tbsp. mushrooms
- Mexican spice to taste
- chili powder to taste
- Himalayan crystal salt
- pepper to taste
- pure water as needed
- ½ c. dried corn
- ½ tbsp. dried mushrooms

Directions

In a blender, puree corn, tomatoes, onion, zucchini, garlic, and spices until creamy. Add water as necessary to achieve the desired thickness.

Place soup on a nonstick dryer sheet and dehydrate, halfway through, flip and break off pieces to powder. Use a food processor or coffee grinder. Place the powder in a bag and label it.

Add dried corn and mushrooms to the bag of powdered mixture for "floaters". In a separate bag, place adzuki beans.

To EAT: Sprout the adzuki beans **3 DAYS AHEAD.**

Put the sprouted beans in a bowl. Add about 2-4 cups of water to the powdered mixture in a separate bowl and let the powder sit for about 20 minutes. Stir it to make sure it is well mixed. Start with less water and if needed, add more water until the desired thickness is achieved. Add the sprouted beans to soup. Enjoy!

NOTE: May warm to 100°F if desired.

Creamed Cauliflower Soup

Makes 4-6 Servings

Ingredients

- 1 head cauliflower
- 1 carrot, shredded
- 2 stocks celery
- 1 c. cashews
- 1 tsp. turmeric
- 1 tsp. Himalayan crystal salt
- ¼ tsp. pepper
- 1 c. young coconut, meat
- dash paprika (optional)

Directions

Wash and chop cauliflower and place in a blender. To the blender add carrot, celery, cashews, young coconut meat, and water. Add the turmeric, salt, and pepper blend until creamy.

Place soup on a nonstick sheet and dry. Halfway through the drying process, flip it and remove nonstick sheet.

Once the soup is dehydrated, break off pieces and powder it either in a food processor or coffee grinder. Place the powder in a bag and label it.

To EAT: Add about 2-4 cups of water and let sit for about 20 minutes. Stir it to make sure it is well mixed. Start with less water and as needed, add water as desired.

Place in a bowl and garnish with pickled cauliflower or sprinkle with paprika if desired.

Rabbits Carrot Soup

Makes 4-6 Servings

Ingredients

- 3 c. carrots, shredded
- 2 stalks celery, chopped
- 1 c. cashews or macadamia nuts
- 1 tbsp. cold pressed olive oil
- ¼ c. onion, chopped
- 2 tbsp. garlic powder
- 2 lemons, juiced
- pinch ginger
- water as needed
- Himalayan crystal salt to taste
- pepper to taste

Directions

Put celery and carrots in a blender add the remaining ingredients, adding water to achieve the desired thickness.

Place soup on a nonstick sheet to dry. Flip the soup halfway through the drying process and remove the nonstick sheet, place directly on the dryer shelf. Once the soup is completely dry, break off pieces and powder it in a food processor or coffee grinder. Pour the powder in a bag and label it.

Option: Add dried carrots to the powdered mix for "floaters."

To EAT: Add about 2-4 cups of water and let sit for about 20 minutes. Stir to make sure it is well mixed. Start with less water and add more water as needed.

Apple Parsnip Soup

Makes 2-4 Servings

Ingredients

- 2 green onions, chopped
- 3 celery stocks, sliced
- 4 medium apples, chopped
- 4 parsnips
- 1 tsp. parsley
- ¼ c. cashews or macadamia nuts
- water as needed
- Himalayan crystal salt taste
- pepper to taste

Directions

In a blender, combine green onions, celery, apples, parsnips, and nuts until smooth. Add only enough water to obtain desired thickness.

Place soup on a nonstick sheet and dry. Flipping and removing the nonstick sheet halfway through.

Once soup is completely dry. Break off pieces and powder it either in food processor or coffee grinder. Place the powder in a bag and label it.

To EAT: Add about 2-4 cups of water and let sit for about 20 minutes. Stir to make sure it is well mixed. Start with less water and add more as needed.

Corn Chowder

Makes 2-4 Servings

Ingredients

- 4 tbsp. onion powder
- 1 ½ c. corn,
- ¼ c. nut milk (page 71)
- ¼ c. dried peas
- ¼ c. dried carrots
- ¼ c. dried corn
- ½ c. rutabaga or turnip
- ¼ tsp. thyme
- ¼ tsp. turmeric
- Himalayan crystal salt to taste

Directions

In a blender, combine onion, corn, thyme, turmeric, salt and nut seed milk.

Place soup on a nonstick sheet start to dry. Flip it halfway and remove the nonstick drying sheet.

Once soup is completely dry. Break off pieces and powder it either in food processor or coffee grinder. Place the powder in a bag and label it.

In a separate bag, place the dried peas, carrots, corn and rutabaga (or turnip if using).

To EAT: Soak the vegetables for 20 minutes. Then drain off extra liquid.

Soak the soup powder for about 20 minutes in a bowl. Pour over peas, carrots, corn and rutabaga. Add salt and pepper to taste, until the desired thickness is achieved.

Carrot Ginger Soup

Makes 4-6 Servings

Ingredients

- 1 ½ c. carrot, grated
- 1 tbsp. ginger
- 1 tbsp. garlic powder
- 1 lemon, juiced
- 1 tbsp. cold pressed olive oil
- water as needed

Directions

Combine carrots, ginger, garlic, lemon juice, and olive oil in a blender until creamy. Add water as necessary to achieve the desired thickness.

Place the soup on a nonstick sheet and dry. Flipping and removing the nonstick sheet halfway through.

Once soup is dehydrated. Break off pieces and powder it either in a food processor or coffee grinder. Place the powder in a bag and label it.

Option: Add freeze-dried carrots to the powdered mixture for floaters.

To EAT: Add about 2-4 cups of water and let sit for about 20 minutes. Stir it to make sure it is well mixed. Start with less water and add more water as desired.

Vegetable 'Noodle' Soup

Makes 4-6 Servings

Ingredients

Soup Base

- 1 c. pure water
- ½ c. celery
- ¼ c. onion
- ¼ tsp. poultry seasoning
- 2 tsp. Himalayan crystal salt
- ½ tsp. black pepper

"Noodles"

- ¾ c. celery, sliced
- ¾ c. carrot, shredded
- ¾ c. zucchini, shredded
- ½ c. corn, taken off the cob

Directions

In a blender, puree water, celery, onion, and seasoning in a blender until creamy. Add water as necessary to achieve the desired thickness.

Place soup on a nonstick sheet and dry. Flipping and removing the nonstick sheet halfway through.

Once the soup is dehydrated. Break off pieces and powder it either in a food processor or coffee grinder. Place the powder in a bag and label it.

Slice celery, shred carrot and zucchini, and dry fresh-cut corn kernels. Dry completely.

Once the vegetables are dry, store them—for future "noodles" --in separate bags.

To EAT: Put the veggie "noodles" in a bowl and soak for 20 minutes. In a separate bowl, soak the soup base powder. Add about 2-4 cups of water to the powdered mixture and let sit for about 20 minutes. Stir it to make sure it is well mixed. Start with less water, as more as desired, and then pour the liquid over the noodles.

Vegetable Soup Base

Makes 2-4 Servings

Ingredients

- ½ c. onion
- 1 c. turnip
- 1 c. parsnip
- 8 c. celery
- 1 zucchini, diced
- Himalayan crystal salt
- pepper to taste

Directions

Combine onion, carrots, turnip, parsnip, and celery in a blender.

Pour mixture into "milk bag" or a clean nylon knee high and strain over a bowl.

Squeeze to make sure all the liquid is out. Add the spice to the juice and let set for at least an hour. Store it in a container and refrigerate.

Either use in other recipes before drying or dry and powder for later use.

Mexican Vegetable Soup

Makes 4-6 Servings

Ingredients

- ½ yellow or orange bell pepper, diced
- 1 red bell pepper, diced
- 1 tbsp. ground cumin
- ½ tsp. dried oregano
- ¼ tsp. cayenne pepper
- ¼ c. red onion, finely chopped
- ½ c. zucchini, chopped
- 1 tbsp. jalapeno pepper, diced
- 2 c. vegetable soup base
- 1 c. corn kernels
- 1 zucchini, diced
- Himalayan crystal salt to taste
- pepper to taste

Optional Toppings

- lime juice
- cilantro
- sour cream

Directions

Make and dry vegetable soup base (page 64) and place in a labeled bag with cumin, oregano, cayenne pepper, salt, and pepper. and spices.

Prepare bell peppers, red onion, jalapeno, zucchini, corn, salt, place on a nonstick sheet and dry. Place the dried vegetables in a bag and label it.

To EAT: Soak vegetable base and vegetables in about 2-4 cups of water and let it sit for about 20 minutes. Stir to make sure it is well mixed. Start with less water and add more water as desired. Add any optional toppings. Serve immediately.

Yellow Pepper Tomato Soup

Makes 2-4 Servings

Ingredients

- ½ c. dried tomatoes, soaked in water
- 1 onion, chopped
- 1 clove garlic
- 3 yellow bell peppers
- 4 large tomatoes
- 1 ½ tsp. dried thyme
- 2 tsp. paprika
- 1 pinch ground cayenne pepper
- Himalayan crystal salt to taste
- pepper to taste
- sour cream optional garnish
- tender green sprouts

Directions

Barely cover dried tomatoes with pure water, soak for 15 minutes. Place tomatoes in a blender with soaking water.

Wash and cut fresh tomatoes then place them in the blender.

Cut and seed the bell peppers, add them to the blender along with chopped onion, garlic and the spices. Blend until smooth.

Place soup on a nonstick sheet and dry. Flip and remove the nonstick sheet halfway through.

Once the soup is completely dry, break off pieces and powder it either in food processor or coffee grinder. Place the powder in a bag and label it.

To EAT: Add about 2-4 cups of water and let sit for about 20 minutes. Stir until it is well mixed, adding more water as needed.

Place in soup bowls and garnish with sour cream and/or tender green sprouts.

Italian Tomato Soup

Makes 4-6 Servings

Ingredients

- 1 c. dried tomatoes, soaked 15 minutes in pure water
- 6 fresh tomatoes
- ½ tbsp. Italian seasoning
- 2-3 green onions
- 1-2 zucchinis
- 1 yellow squash
- 2-4 cloves garlic
- Himalayan crystal salt to taste
- pepper to taste
- sunflower greens, for garnish

Directions

Soak dried tomatoes in water for about 20 minutes. Remove tomatoes and place them in a blender. Add the 6 fresh tomatoes, seasonings, green onions, zucchini, and yellow squash. Blend into a soup.

Place soup on a nonstick sheet and dry. Flip and remove the nonstick sheet halfway through.

Once the soup is completely dry, break off pieces and powder it either in food processor or coffee grinder. Place the powder in a bag and label it.

To EAT: Add about 2-4 cups of water and let sit for about 20 minutes. Stir until it is well mixed, adding more water as needed. Add sunflower greens for a garnish.

Kale Soup

Makes 4-6 Servings

Ingredients

- 1 onion
- 1 clove garlic
- ¼ tsp. red pepper flakes
- 1 ½ c. jicama, peeled and cubed
- 1 bunch kale, with stem removed
- 3 c. vegetable base

Directions

Make Vegetable Soup Base. Before drying it use it in this recipe.

Remove the stems from the kale and tear into bite-sized pieces.

Peel the jicama then cut into ¼ inch cubes. Place the jicama in a bowl along with the onion, garlic, kale, red pepper flakes and vegetable base blend until smooth.

Place the soup on a nonstick sheet and dry. Flipping and removing the nonstick sheet halfway through.

Once soup is completely dry. Break off pieces and powder it either in food processor or coffee grinder. Place the powder in a bag and label it.

Place dried the peas, carrots, corn and rutabaga or turnip if using dried in a separate bag.

To EAT: Add about 2-4 cups of water to powdered and vegetables for about 20 minutes. Stir until it is well mixed, adding more water as needed. Garnish with sprouts or kale chips.

Parsnip Chowder

Makes 2-4 Servings

Ingredients

- 1 c. carrots, diced
- 1 c. jicama, diced
- 2 c. parsnips, diced
- 1 ½ c. onion, diced
- 1 ½ c. almond milk (page 71)
- ½ c. almond pulp
- 1 tsp. Himalayan crystal salt
- ½ tsp. pepper
- ½ tsp. turmeric

Directions

Peel parsnips then dice along with carrots, jicama, and onion. Place in a blender, add salt, pepper, and turmeric. Blend until smooth.

Pour almond milk in the blender; add almond pulp and blend until smooth. If it is too thin, add more almond pulp.

Pour soup on a nonstick sheet and dry. Halfway through the drying process, flip drying soup, and carefully place it on the drying shelf. Continue the drying process.

If floaters are desired add shredded and dried carrots and jicama to soup mix.

Once soup is dehydrated, break off pieces and powder it either in a food processor or a coffee grinder. Place the powder in a bag and label it.

To EAT: Add about 2-4 cups of water and let sit for about 20 minutes. Stir it to make sure it is well mixed. Add more water as needed.

TIP: To add color, use freeze-dried carrots to float on the top.

Chili Stew

Makes 4-6 Servings

Ingredients

- 2 c. tomatoes, soaked in pure water
- ¼ c. mushrooms, ground then
- 3 tbsp. hot peppers, if desired
- 2 garlic cloves
- ¼ c. lemon or lime, juice
- ½ tsp. celery seed
- ½ tsp. chili powder or more
- 1 ½ tsp. mustard seed, ground
- pinch cayenne pepper
- ¼ tsp. coriander, ground
- 1 ½ c red bell pepper, chopped
- 2 c. dried corn
- 1 c. dried zucchini, chopped
- pure water to desired thickness

Directions

In a blender, combine tomatoes, mushrooms, hot peppers, garlic, lemon juice, celery seed, chili powder, mustard seed, cayenne pepper, coriander, and one cup corn until smooth.

Place soup on a nonstick sheet and dry. Halfway through, flip and take off the nonstick sheet, continue drying.

Once soup is completely dry. Break off pieces and powder it either in food processor or coffee grinder. Place the powder in a bag and label it.

In separate bag place dried bell peppers, dried zucchini, dried mushrooms, and one cup of dried corn.

To EAT: Add about 2-4 cups of water to powdered soup and vegetables for about 20 minutes. Stir until it is well mixed, adding more water as needed. May warm to 100°F if desired.

Cool Cucumber Soup

Makes 2 cups

Ingredients

- 2 medium cucumbers
- ½ small onion
- 3 celery stocks
- 1 tbsp. raw apple cider vinegar
- 2 tsp. Himalayan crystal salt
- water as needed

Directions

Blend all ingredients in a blender until smooth. Adding only enough water for blender to work.

Place soup on a nonstick sheet and dry. Halfway through the dehydrating, flip and place the drying soup on the dehydration rack, and remove the nonstick sheet.

Once soup is completely dry. Break off pieces and powder it in a food processor or coffee grinder. Place the powder in a bag and label it.

To EAT: Soak soup powder for about 20 minutes. Pour over the reserved vegetables. May warm to 100°F if desired.

Chapter 11
Food Storage Recipes

The following recipes can be made from food that you have stored or grown.

Almond Milk

Makes 2 cups

Ingredients
- 1 c. almonds (soaked overnight)
- 2 c. pure water

Directions
Place almonds in blender with water and blend. Pour the mixture out into a milk bag (may use cheesecloth or clean nylon sock) and squeeze the liquid out creating milk. You may want to sweeten the milk.

If you don't have power use a hand or bicycle blender.

Reserve left over pulp for use in other recipes.

May use any variety of nuts to make milk hazelnut, Brazil nuts, and etcetera.

Frosty Drink

Makes 2 cups

Ingredients
- 2 c. almond milk
- ¼ c. raw liquid sweetener
- 4 tbsp. raw carob powder or powdered freeze-dried berries

Directions
Place almond milk, carob or powdered berries, and sweetener in blender mix until it is thick and smooth. BLEND and enjoy!

Hibiscus Drink

Makes 2 cups

Ingredients

- ½ c. dried hibiscus flowers
- ½ tsp. ground cinnamon
- ½ tsp. ground cloves
- ¼ tsp. allspice, crushed
- 1 tbsp. dried ginger
- ½ c. dried apples
- 5 c. water
- ½ c. raw liquid sweetener (optional)

Directions

Used dried apples that have been powdered or apples from root cellar, mix in cloves, allspice, cinnamon, and ginger place in a glass jar along with hibiscus flowers. Fill the jar with water and place in the sun for 4-6 hours.

Strain hibiscus drink into a pitcher and chill.

This is a tangy drink. If you would like it sweeter, add as much sweetener as needed. Serve the drink over ice and use a hibiscus flower or cinnamon stick as garnish.

Rejuvelac

Makes 2 cups

Ingredients

- 1 c. sprouted wheat, ½ -1 inch tail
- 1 gallon water

Directions

THREE DAYS PRIOR:
Sprout the wheat for one to three days. The wheat should have a ½ to 1 inch sprouted tail.

Drain the soaking water and place wheat in a food processor. Add 2 cups of pure water and pulse the blender for 2-3 minutes until everything is well blended.

Pour into a gallon pitcher and add the remaining water. Stir the liquid and then cover with cheesecloth.

Stir the liquid 2 to 4 times a day for 2 to 3 days. Refrigerate after the fermentation time. You should have a slightly lemony flavor when done. If it stinks, it is no good and can be put in the mulch.

Note

This fermented product is good for the digestion having friendly flora for the intestines. Some people drink rejuvelac straight from the refrigerator and love it.

Fun Fact

"Rejuvelac" is a general term for a fermented liquid used to improve digestion. Rejuvelac can be made with grains using; whole wheat, rye, quinoa, oats, barley, millet, buckwheat, rice, or other types of grain. Best results have been found using wheat, rye, and quinoa.

Greek Dressing

Makes about ½ cup

Ingredients

- 4 tbsp. cold pressed olive oil
- 5 tbsp. powdered lemon
- ½ c. water
- 1 tsp. oregano, dried
- 1 tsp. parsley
- 1 tsp. garlic powder
- 1 tsp. basil, dried
- 1 tsp. onion powder
- ½ tsp. black pepper, ground

Directions

Place powered lemon in water for 20 minutes, this becomes lemon juice.

In a small bowl, mix olive oil, lemon juice, oregano, garlic powder, onion powder, basil, black pepper, and parsley. Enjoy on salad of microgreens.

Fiesta Dressing

Makes about ½ cup

Ingredients

- 4 tbsp. cold pressed olive oil
- 2 tbsp. raw apple cider vinegar
- 1 tsp. onion powder
- 5 tbsp. powdered lemon
- ½ c. water
- Himalayan crystal salt to taste
- white pepper to taste

Directions

In a jar with a screw top, combine powdered lime, ginger, and garlic, place lid on the jar and shake well. Chill dressing until serving time.

Shake dressing well before pouring over the salad.

Lemon Dill Dressing

Makes about ½ cup

Ingredients

- 2 tbsp. dill, chopped
- 2 tsp. lemon, powder
- 1 tsp. mustard seed, ground
- ¼ c. cold pressed olive oil
- ¼ tsp. Himalayan crystal salt
- ¼ tsp. black pepper
- 3 tbsp. water

Directions

Place powered lemon in water for 20 minutes, this becomes lemon juice.

In a small bowl or jar with tight lid combine lemon juice, dill, mustard seed, olive oil, salt, and pepper.

Italian Dressing

Makes ½ cup

Ingredients

- 3 tbsp. cold pressed olive oil
- 1 tsp. raw apple cider vinegar
- ½ tsp. dried parsley
- 1 tsp. lemon powder
- 4 tbsp. water
- ½ tsp. garlic powder
- ½ tsp. dried basil
- ¼ tsp. crushed red pepper
- ½ tsp. dried oregano

Directions

Place powered lemon in water for 20 minutes, this becomes lemon juice.

Combine oil, vinegar, parsley, lemon juice, garlic, basil, crushed red pepper, and oregano in small bowl and whisk until well mixed. You can also place the ingredients in a jar with a lid and mix it that way.

Eggless Salad

Makes 4-6 Servings

Ingredients

- 2 c. sesame seed pulp, saved from making sesame milk
- ½ c. dried red bell pepper, finely chopped
- ½ c dried carrot, shredded
- 1tbsp. onion powder
- 1 tbsp. parsley
- 1 tbsp. dill
- 1 tsp. mustard seed powder
- 1 tbsp. turmeric
- 2 tsp. lovage
- ¼ c. nut mayo (page 107)
- Himalayan crystal salt to taste

Directions

DAY BEFORE: Make sesame milk or soak the sesame seeds overnight, and drain water off.

Soak dried bell pepper and carrot for about 20 minutes.

In a bowl, mix sesame seeds, bell pepper, carrot, onion, parsley, dill, and mustard seed powder, turmeric, lovage, and salt with nut mayo.

Enjoy this refreshing salad on top of the microgreens you grew!

Fun Fact

Lovage--is a relatively unknown perennial herb. The flavor of lovage is strong, so only a few plants are required for the herb garden.

Sprout Salad

Makes 4-6 Servings

Ingredients

- 1 c. mung bean spouts
- 1 c. mixed microgreens
- 1 c. other tender green (optional)
- Italian dressing to taste

Directions

THREE DAYS AHEAD: Sprout mung beans and microgreens until greens are growing.

On a plate, place tender greens--if using them, or place half of the bean sprouts on one third of the plate. Then place the microgreens next to the mung beans. Place reaming mung beans next to the microgreens.

Make Italian dressing and pour over salad to taste.

Note

You can use adzuki, bean greens in place of or with the mung beans greens. You can also use pea or sunflower greens.

Microgreen Salad

Makes 2-4 Servings

Ingredients

- 1 c. microgreens
- ¼ c. walnuts, chopped
- ½ c. parsley from herb garden
- 4 tbsp. rawmesan (page 103)
- ½ c. sunflower greens
- 1 c. tender greens if available
- Himalayan crystal salt to taste
- black pepper to taste
- Italian dressing

Directions

Wash and prepare microgreens (and tender greens) and place in a bowl.

Add walnuts, parsley, rawmesan, sunflower greens, pea greens, salt, and pepper and toss. Dress with Italian dressing before serving.

Microgreen Salad with Lime Vinaigrette

Makes 2-4 Servings

Ingredients

- 1 c. microgreens
- 6 radishes, halved or sliced, from garden (optional)
- 2 tbsp. lime juice
- ¼ tsp. dry mustard powder
- ¼ tsp. Himalayan crystal salt
- 4 tbsp. cold pressed olive oil
- ground pepper, to taste

Directions

AHEAD OF TIME: Grow microgreens. When ready to eat, add them to radishes, and toss into a salad bowl.

In a jar, make lime juice by using dried lime powder, and soak the powder in water for 20 minutes. Add mustard, salt, and olive oil place lid on the jar and shake.

Just before serving, dress the salad lightly with dressing, sprinkle with salt and ground pepper.

Fun Fact

Microgreens are bigger than sprouts and "seedlings" and are the greens of edible vegetables and herbs. There are over 25 varieties of microgreens including arugula, basil, beets, kale, and cilantro.

Most microgreens grow in a week or two and when grown indoors, will yield year-round. Microgreens require both soil and sunlight.

Kamut Salad with Vinaigrette

Makes 6-8 Servings

Ingredients

Salad

- 1 c. kamut or wheat berries,
- ¾ c. dried red bell pepper,
- ¾ c. dried yellow bell pepper,
- ¾ c. dried small summer squash, sliced
- ¾ c. dried tomatoes, chopped

Vinaigrette

- 3 tbsp. cold pressed olive oil
- 3 tbsp. raw apple cider vinegar
- 2 tbsp. onion powder
- 1 tbsp. water
- 1 tbsp. mustard powder
- 1 tbsp. garlic powder
- 1 tsp. cayenne pepper
- 1 tsp. thyme
- ½ tsp. Himalayan crystal salt
- black pepper to taste

Directions

THREE DAYS AHEAD: Sprout kamut for 2 or 3 days, until it is soft.

Soak bell peppers, squash, and tomatoes in a large bowl for 20-30 minutes. Drain the soaking water off, add the kumut berries, and set aside.

In a small bowl, combine olive oil, vinegar, onion, mustard, garlic, cayenne pepper, thyme, salt, and pepper with a fork--or whisk until well mixed.

Toss salad with vinaigrette.

'Tuna' Salad

Makes 2-4 Servings

Ingredients

- 1 c. sunflower seeds, soaked
- 1 tsp. onion salt
- Himalayan crystal salt to taste
- 1 tbsp. dried lemon, powdered
- ½ c. dried celery
- 1 tbsp. kelp
- ½ c. nut mayo
- 1 c. microgreens
- other green sprouts

Directions

AHEAD OF TIME: Soak sunflower seeds overnight, after they have finished soaking, they should have almost doubled in volume. Drain the water and rinse seeds.

Place the seeds in a food processor along with celery, onion, salt, lemon powder, and kelp blend. Don't mix it too long--It should have plenty of textures.

Place 'tuna' mixture in a bowl and gently mix in nut mayo with a spoon.

On a plate, place microgreens and then a scoop of 'tuna.' Sprinkle with more kelp and sprouts. Serve and enjoy!

Mixed Sprout Salad

Makes 4-6 Servings

Ingredients

- ½ c. chickpeas, sprouted
- ½ c. mung beans, sprouted
- ½ c. lentils, sprouted
- 1 c. dried carrots, shredded
- ¼ c. dried shallots chopped, or grown in herb garden
- ¼ c. radish sprouts
- 2 tbsp. dried cilantro
- 3 tsp. cayenne pepper
- 1 ½ tab. cold pressed olive oil
- ¾ tsp. mustard powder
- 1 tbsp. ginger powder
- 2 tbsp. lemon juice
- 1 tsp. turmeric
- 2 tsp. red pepper flakes (optional)
- Himalayan crystal salt to taste

Directions

AHEAD OF TIME: Sprout mung beans and chickpeas.

SPROUTING NOTES: Mung beans usually sprout quicker - 6 to 8 hours. Chickpeas may take longer, 12 hours or more. Sprout radishes to small greens about 3-6 days.

Rehydrate carrots and dry shallots (unless using fresh shallots from garden) for 30 minutes in water.

Place sprouted legumes in a bowl, add carrots, shallots, radish sprouts, and cilantro; mix well.

Make lemon juice by placing powdered lemon in water for 20 minutes.

In a small bowl, whisk together lemon juice, olive oil, cayenne pepper, and mustard powder, ginger, salt, turmeric, and red pepper flakes.

Add dressing to the sprouts and combine them well. Garnish with fresh herbs if available.

Layered Taco Salad

Makes 2-4 Servings

Ingredients

- 4 c. tender green sprouts
- ¼ c. raw olives
- sunflower beans (page 91)
- nacho cheese (page 103)
- sour cream (page 105)

Directions

AHEAD OF TIME: Sprout tender greens, such as microgreens.

Make taco meat, cheese and sour cream.

On a plate, layer tender greens, sunflower beans, nacho cheese, olives and finely sour cream.

Wild Rice and Microgreen Salad

Makes 4-6 Servings

Ingredients

- ¾ c. wild rice, sprouted
- ¼ c. chopped flat leaf parsley (from herb garden or 2 tbsp. dried)
- ¼ c. chopped mint leafs
- 2 tbsp. chopped dill
- ½ c. microgreen sprouts
- ¼ c. almonds, chopped
- ½ tsp. onion powder
- Himalayan crystal salt to taste
- black pepper to taste
- 2 tbsp. lemon juice
- 2 tbsp. cold pressed olive oil

Directions

AHEAD OF TIME: Sprout rice and microgreens

Toss together rice, microgreens, parsley, mint, dill, and almonds.

Make lemon juice by placing powdered lemon in water for 20 minutes.

In a bowl, mix the olive oil, onion powder, salt and pepper, and lemon juice, and then toss with the salad before serving.

Mung Sprouts Salad

Makes 2-4 Servings

Ingredients

- ½ c. mung beans, sprouted
- ½ c. almonds, soaked
- 1 tsp. onions powder
- 4 tbsp. mint leaves few
- Himalayan crystal salt to taste
- 1 tbsp. lemon powder
- ¼ c. water
- 1 tsp. dried cucumber chopped
- ½ c. microgreens or other tender green sprouts

> **Fun Fact**
>
> Herbs are plant leaves while spices are every other part of the plant.

Directions

AHEAD OF TIME: Sprout mung beans and microgreens. Soak almonds overnight, drain water off then chop nuts. Place chopped nuts in a bowl.

Place powdered lemon in water for 20 minutes, this becomes lemon juice.

Soak cucumber for about 20 minutes to rehydrate. Add to mung beans, nuts, mint and microgreens. Dress salad with lemon juice, onion powder and salt, toss salad.

Sprouted Soup

Makes 4-6 Servings

Ingredients

- 1-2 c. mixed spouts, such as adzuki beans, peas, lentils, mung beans, triticale, wheat, fenugreek, sprouted
- ½ c. dried carrot, chopped
- ½ c. dried celery, chopped
- ¼ c. dried onion, chopped
- 2 tbsp. garlic powder
- 1 c. dried red bell pepper, chopped
- ¾ c. dried tomatoes, chopped
- Himalayan crystal salt to taste
- 2 ½ tsp. poultry seasoning
- 1 c. microgreen sprouts

Directions

AHEAD OF TIME: Sprout bean mix and microgreen seeds.

Rehydrate carrots, celery, onion, bell pepper and tomatoes for 20 minutes.

Drain water off of vegetables and place in a bowl then mix in the sprouts and seasoning adding enough of the vegetable soaking water to make it the consistency that you wish it to be. May warm if desired.

Wild Rice Chowder

Makes 4-6 Servings

Ingredients

- 7 dried mushrooms, sliced
- 1 stalk celery, thinly sliced
- 1 tsp. Himalayan crystal salt
- ½ tsp. mustard seed powder
- 3 tbsp. hot pepper, minced
- ½ c. almonds, soaked overnight
- 3 tbsp. onion
- ½ tsp. poultry seasoning
- pepper to taste
- pinch of paprika
- 3 c. wild rice
- sprouts, (optional)

Directions

3 DAYS BEFORE: Sprout wild rice. Rice is ready when soft and easy to chew.

Soak dried mushrooms for 20 minutes. Remove from water and place in a blender.

In a blender, combine mushrooms, celery, almonds, salt, hot pepper, onion, poultry seasoning, paprika, and pepper until smooth--adding water if needed to reach desired texture.

Serve over sprouted rice and garnish with tender green plants (sprouts such as pea greens, sunflower, or a mixture of greens).

Dirty Rice

Makes 2-4 Servings

Ingredients

- 1 tsp. cold pressed olive oil
- ½ c. dried onion, chopped
- 1 stalk dried celery,
- ½ c. dried red bell pepper, chopped
- 1 tbsp. garlic powder
- 3 c. wild rice, sprouted
- 1 ½ c. sprouts (such as adzuki beans, green peas, lentils, mung beans, fenugreek, triticale, wheat)
- 1 tbsp. thyme
- 1 tsp. cumin, ground
- ½ tsp. cayenne pepper
- ¼ c. water
- 2 tbsp. lime powder
- Himalayan crystal salt to taste

Directions

AHEAD OF TIME: Sprout rice and other sprouts.

Soak lime powder in water for 20 minutes, lime juice is now ready. To lime juice add salt, cayenne pepper, cumin, thyme, and garlic powder whisk well.

Soak onion, celery and peppers in water for 20 minutes. Drain off water.

In a large bowl, mix rice, spouts, onion, and pepper, stir in lime dressing. May warm to 100°F.

Cardamom Rice

Makes 4-6 Servings

Ingredients

- ¼ c. dried cauliflower
- ¼ c. dried squash
- ¼ c. dried broccoli
- 1-2 tbsp. garlic, minced
- ¼ c. onion, diced
- 1 tsp. curry powder
- 1-2 tsp. turmeric
- 6 c. wild rice, sprouted
- 1 tsp. cardamom seeds, soaked overnight
- 2 c. dried red bell peppers
- 1 ½ tbsp. cold pressed olive oil
- 3 tbsp. water if needed

Directions

AHEAD OF TIME: Sprout rice until tender about 3 days.

Soak cauliflower, squash, broccoli, and onion in water for 20 minutes. Soak bell pepper in separate bowl.

In a blender, combine red bell pepper and olive oil until smooth, adding bell pepper soaking water as needed to thin.

Serve with vegetables and rice next to each other on a plate. Pour sauce next to the vegetables.

Lemon Rice

Makes 2-4 Servings

Ingredients

- 2 c. wild rice, sprouted
- ¼ c. dried onion, finely chopped
- 2 tsp. cold pressed olive oil
- 2 tbsp. dried lemon
- ¼ c. water
- ¼ tsp. Himalayan crystal salt
- 1 c. dried parsley, chopped
- ½ c. kale sprouts
- ¾ c. dried broccoli, chopped

> **Fun Fact**
>
> The leaves of a lemon tree can be used to make tea.

Directions

AHEAD OF TIME: Sprout rice until tender about 3 days, and kale for tender greens

Soak onion and broccoli for 20 minutes.

Make lemon juice from grinding the dry lemon to powder and then soaking in water for 20 minutes.

In a bowl, combine rice, onion, olive oil, lemon juice, salt, parsley, broccoli, and kale by hand until well mixed. Set aside to allow the flavors to mingle. May warm if desired.

Wild Jambalaya

Makes 4-6 Servings

Ingredients

- 2 c. wild rice, sprouted

Sauce

- 1-2 cloves garlic
- 1 tsp. oregano, dried
- 1 tbsp. parsley, dried
- 1 tsp. thyme, dried
- ¼ tsp. cayenne
- dash paprika
- ½ tsp. pepper
- ½ tsp. Himalayan crystal salt
- ½ c. sun-dried tomatoes

Vegetables

- 1 c. dried red bell pepper, chopped
- 1 c. dried onion, chopped
- 1 c. dried zucchini, chopped
- ½ c. dried celery, chopped
- 1 c. dried broccoli florets

Directions

AHEAD OF TIME: Sprout rice until tender about 3 days. The rice is ready to eat when it is soft and easy to chew.

Soak dried tomatoes for 20 minutes in just enough pure water to cover. Place in a blender with the water and add garlic powder, oregano, parsley, thyme, cayenne pepper, paprika, pepper, and salt mix until well combined.

Soak the dried bell pepper, onion, zucchini, celery and broccoli in water for about 30 minutes. Drain off the water and place in a bowl with the wild rice.

Pour sauce over the rice and mix. Garnish with fresh herbs from herb garden.

Creamy Mustard with Vegetables

Makes 4-6 Servings

Ingredients

Vegetables

- 1 tsp. cold pressed olive oil
- 2-4 tsp. garlic powder
- ¼ c. onion powder
- 1 c. dried red bell peppers, chopped
- 1 c. dried yellow summer squash, shredded
- 1 c. dried zucchini, shredded
- 1 tbsp. chives, finely chopped

Sauce

- ½ c. cashews
- ½ c. water
- 4 tbsp. lemon powder
- 3 tbsp. mustard powder
- 1 tbsp. cold pressed olive oil
- ½ c. water

Directions

Soak bell peppers, summer squash, and zucchini for 20 minutes in water. Drain water and place vegetables in a bowl. Add chives, olive oil, garlic, and onion powders mix and set aside.

Soak lemon powder in water for 20 minutes then place in a blender.

To lemon juice in the blender, add cashews, mustard powder, and olive oil. Combine until creamy, adding vegetable soaking water as needed.

Combine sauce and vegetables and let flavors mingle for at least an hour.

Note

If no blender is available, use a mortar and pestle to grind the nuts, then whisk the remaining ingredients together.

Warm Mexi-Rice

Makes 4-6 Servings

Ingredients

- 2 c. organic wild rice, sprouted
- ¼ c. dried onion, chopped
- ½ c. dried red bell pepper, chopped
- 3 tbsp. hot pepper chopped
- ¼ c. dried tomatoes
- 2 tbsp. chili powder
- 2 tsp. Himalayan crystal salt
- 1 tsp. turmeric

Directions

AHEAD OF TIME: Sprout rice for 3 days.

When ready to eat; soak onion, bell pepper, hot pepper and tomatoes in water for 20 minutes.

In a bowl, combine rice, onion, bell pepper, hot pepper, tomatoes, chili powder, salt, and turmeric make sure everything is coated. May warm in a pan or dehydrator to 100°F.

Kale Burger

Makes 4-6 Servings

Ingredients

- 2 c. almonds, soaked
- 1 c. dried carrots, shredded
- 2 tbsp. lemon, juiced
- 1 tbsp. garlic powder
- 1 dried tomatoes
- 1 c. dried corn
- 1 dried red bell pepper,
- 4 tbsp. dried parsley
- 1 c. dried kale
- 1 c. dried zucchini
- 1 c. dried broccoli
- 1 tbsp. ground celery seed
- ½ tbsp. poultry seasoning
- 2 tbsp. dried onion
- ½ c. raw tahini
- 1 tbsp. slippery elm powder
- 1 tbsp. cold pressed olive oil
- Himalayan crystal salt to taste

Directions

NIGHT BEFORE: Soak almonds overnight, drain off water, and set aside.

Soak dried carrots, tomatoes, corn, red bell pepper, kale, zucchini, broccoli, and onion for 30 minutes.

Make lemon juice from grinding dry lemon to powder and then soaking in water for 20 minutes.

In a food processor, combine almonds, carrots, tomatoes, corn, red bell pepper, parsley, kale, zucchini, broccoli, lemon juice, tahini, garlic, olive oil, and spices until mixed thoroughly. If doing it by hand, grind nuts in a mortar and pestle and then add the other ingredients.

Shape into burgers and dehydrate on nonstick dehydrator sheets for 2-4 hours. Flip and carefully remove the nonstick dehydrator sheet. Continue drying for another 2-4 hours.

Serve on tender greens and with any other fresh garden vegetables available.

Note

If no power is available, use a sun dryer or serve as is on a plate.

Fun Fact

Slippery elm is a glue-like substance found in the inner bark of slippery elm tree has long been steeped in water as a remedy for throat ailments, powdered for use in poultices, and chewed on as a thirst quencher, among other health uses.

Falafel Patties

Makes 6-8 Servings

Ingredients

- 2 c. garbanzo beans
- ½ c. oat groats, ground in coffee grinder
- 1 tsp. garlic salt
- 2 tbsp. poultry seasoning
- Himalayan crystal salt
- black pepper to taste
- 2 tbsp. water
- 1 tsp. cold pressed olive oil
- 1 tsp. turmeric
- 1 tsp. lemon powder
- 2 tsp. dried parsley or if you have it in your garden a handful of fresh.

Directions

AHEAD OF TIME: Sprout garbanzo beans--soak them overnight then sprout for 3-4 days.

Grind oat groats in coffee grinder then place in food processor. To food processor, add garbanzo beans, garlic, seasoning, olive oil, lemon powder, and parsley. Blend ingredients until smooth, adding water if needed.

Shape mixture into patties about ½" thick. Place on a nonstick dehydrator sheet and dry 1-2 hours at 100°F. Turn patties and continue drying another hour or until the patties reach the desired dryness.

Lasagna

Makes 6-8 Servings

Ingredients

- ricotta cheese sauce (page 100, optional)
- ground meatless

Noodles

- 2 c. dried zucchini, sliced

Veggies

- 1 c. dried yellow squash, chopped
- 1 c. dried yellow bell pepper, chopped
- 1 c. dried red bell pepper, chopped
- ½ c. dried broccoli florets

Marinara Sauce

- 1 c. dried tomatoes
- 1 tsp. cold pressed olive oil
- ½ c. water
- 1 tsp. basil
- 1 tsp. oregano
- 2 tsp. Himalayan crystal salt
- 2-3 tsp dried garlic
- 2 tbsp. dried onion

Directions

AHEAD OF TIME: Soak almonds overnight, drain off water, and set aside.

Soak dried carrots, tomatoes, corn, red bell pepper, kale, zucchini, broccoli, and onion for 30 minutes. Make ground Meatless and Cheese Sauce and set aside.

Soak dried tomatoes in one small bowl. In a different bowl, soak yellow squash, bell pepper, and broccoli for 20 minutes. Set aside.

Prepare marinara sauce. place dried tomatoes and soaking water in a blender along with olive oil, basil, oregano, salt, garlic, and onion until smooth.

In a glass lasagna pan, layer zucchini, vegetables, ground meatless, marinara sauce and ricotta cheese sauce. Continue to layer until all food is used. Place in a dehydrator for about 60 minutes or until warm.

Note

If no blender is available, crush the dried tomatoes to powder before soaking then add remaining ingredients.

Ground Meatless

Makes 6-8 Servings

Ingredients

- 2 c. walnuts, soaked
- 1 tsp. poultry seasoning
- 1 tsp. Italian seasoning
- 1 tsp. garlic salt
- 2 tbsp. onion powder
- ½ tsp. Himalayan crystal salt

Directions

AHEAD OF TIME: Soak walnuts overnight. Drain water and place walnuts in a food processor. Add poultry seasoning, Italian seasoning, garlic, onion, and salt mix until it is chunky and looks a little like ground meat.

Bean Burrito

Makes 4-6 Servings

Ingredients

Crust

- 1 ½ c. dried tomatoes, soaked
- 1 tsp. garlic powder
- 2 tsp. Himalayan crystal salt
- ½ c. flax, ground in a coffee grinder
- 1 tbsp. onion powder
- 1 small dried hot pepper, chopped

Filling

- sunflower beans (page 91)
- sour cream (page 105)
- sprouts for garnish

Directions

In a food processor, mix tomatoes, garlic, salt, flax seed, onion, and hot pepper until looks like dough. If no power is available, crush the tomatoes into a powder then combine in a bowl adding water to combine and make the dough.

Spread on dehydrator nonstick dehydrator sheets in the shape of tacos and dry for about 2-4 hours. Turn the crust over, spread with sunflower beans and roll. Continue drying for about 2-6 hours until desired texture is achieved. Serve on sprouts or microgreens. Drizzle sour cream over the top.

Sunflower Beans

Makes 6-8 Servings

Ingredients

- 2 ½ c. sunflower seeds, soaked
- ¼ c. cold pressed olive oil
- 3 ½ tsp. onion powder
- 1 tbsp. chili powder
- 2 tsp. cumin seed powder
- 1 tsp. Himalayan crystal salt
- 1 tbsp. raw apple cider vinegar
- water if needed

> **Fun Fact**
>
> There are two main types of sunflower crops; one grown for the seeds you eat, while the other is grown for the oil.

Directions

AHEAD OF TIME: Soak sunflower seeds overnight. Drain water off.

Soak bell pepper for about 20 minutes, drain the water and save if needed to make the mixture smooth.

In a food processor, puree sunflower seeds, olive oil, vinegar, onion, chili, cumin, and salt until creamy, add water if needed to reach desired texture.

If food processor is unavailable, crush seeds into a paste by hand then add the remaining ingredients. Mix until smooth, adding water as needed.

Anytime Breakfast Burrito

Makes 4-6 Servings

Ingredients

Crust

- 1 ½ c. dried tomatoes, soaked
- 1 tsp. garlic powder
- 2 tsp. Himalayan crystal salt
- ½ c. flax, ground in a coffee grinder
- ¼ c. onion, chopped
- 1 small hot pepper, seeded and chopped

Filling

- eggless salad (page 76)
- garnish: sour cream and sprouts

Directions

In a coffee grinder, grind the whole flaxseed. for flax meal. Soak tomatoes in water for 20 minutes.

In a food processor, mix garlic, salt, flaxseed, onion, hot pepper, and tomatoes, which have been drained. Mix until it looks like dough. If more moisture is needed, use water that the tomatoes were soaked in.

Spread dough on nonstick dehydrator sheets and dry for about 2-4 hours. Turn crust over; carefully peel off the nonstick dehydrator sheet. Spread with eggless salad and roll.

Continue drying for about 2-6 hours until desired texture is achieved. Serve with sprouts and drizzle sour cream over the top.

Sprouted Pilaf

Makes 2-4 Servings

Ingredients

- 2 c. mixed sprouts, sprouted (such as adzuki beans, green peas, lentils, mung beans, fenugreek, triticale, wheat)
- 1 c. dried, summer squash
- ¼ c. dried onion, chopped
- ½ c. corn kernels, dried or freeze dried
- ½ c. dried peas
- Himalayan crystal salt to taste
- black pepper to taste

Directions

AHEAD OF TIME: Grow sprouts then place in a bowl.

In a separate bowl, soak onion, corn, peas, and squash for about 20 minutes. Drain off the water.

To the vegetables add salt, pepper and sprouts mix and place in a serving dish and enjoy.

May warm if desired.

Taco Pizza

Makes 2-4 Servings

Ingredients

Crust
- 1 c. golden flax seed, ground in a coffee grinder
- 1 c. buckwheat, soaked
- 1 tbsp. Himalayan crystal salt
- 1-2 c. pure water
- ¼ c. raw coconut flour (optional)

Topping
- ½ c. sun dried olives
- ½ c. sunflower beans (page 91)
- 1 c. microgreens
- 1 c. nut mayo (mage 71)

Marinara Sauce
- 1 c. dried tomatoes,
- ½ c. cold pressed olive oil
- 1 tsp. basil
- 1 tsp. oregano
- 2 tsp. Himalayan crystal salt
- 2 tsp. garlic salt
- 1 tbsp. onion powder

Directions

AHEAD OF TIME: Soak buckwheat overnight; drain off water and rinse buckwheat. Put buckwheat in a food processor.

Soak tomatoes in olive oil for 30 minutes then place tomatoes and oil in blender. To blender add basil, oregano, salt, garlic salt, onion powder, and olive oil in a blender and mix.

Grind flax seeds in a coffee grinder and add to the food processor, with the buckwheat and blend. Add salt and only enough water to make dough.

Roll dough out into a circle; use the coconut flour to keep from sticking. (This step could be done with ground flax seed as well.)

Spread sauce on dough. Spread sunflower beans over the sauce. Sprinkle olives over the top with the mayo.

Warm in a dehydrator and set it on 100°F. for an hour or two. Just before serving, cover the top with the microgreen sprouts. Enjoy!

Philly Pizza

Makes 2-4 Servings

Ingredients

Crust

- 1 c. golden flax seed, ground in a coffee grinder
- 1 c. buckwheat, soaked
- 1 tbsp. Himalayan crystal salt
- 1-2 c. pure water
- ¼ c. raw coconut flour (optional)

Mushroom 'Steak'

- 3 dried portobello mushrooms,
- 2 tbsp. cold pressed olive oil
- 2 tbsp. grapefruit powder
- ¼ c. water
- 2 tsp. cumin, ground
- 2 tsp. coriander, ground
- 1 tsp. rosemary, ground
- 1 tsp. celery seed, ground
- 1 tbsp. raw apple cider vinegar

Vegetables

- 1 dried red bell pepper
- 1 dried yellow bell pepper
- 1 dried orange bell pepper
- 1 ½ c. dried broccoli
- 2 tbsp. onion salt
- 1 tsp. garlic powder
- 1 tsp. Himalayan crystal salt
- 1 tsp. savory, ground
- 2 tbsp. cold pressed olive oil

Cheese

- 1 c. sunflower seeds, soaked
- 1 c. pumpkin seeds, soaked
- 3 tbsp. raw apple cider vinegar
- ½ tsp. oregano, dried
- 2 tsp. onion Powder
- 1 tsp. Himalayan crystal salt
- ¼ c. or more water

Directions

AHEAD OF TIME: Make nut mayo and set aside. Soak buckwheat overnight, drain water and rinse buckwheat. Place the buckwheat in a food processor.

Crust

Grind flax in a coffee grinder and place in a food processor, add salt and only enough water to make dough. Roll dough into a circle, using coconut flour to keep from sticking (or use ground flax seed if desired).

Mushroom 'Steak'

Soak grapefruit powder in water for 20 minutes. To grapefruit, add oil, vinegar, cumin, coriander, rosemary, celery seed and vinegar. Slice mushrooms and place in bowl with grapefruit mixture make sure they are well covered. Let marinate while preparing the vegetables.

Vegetables

Put dried peppers and broccoli in a bowl and soak for 20

Continued on next page

minutes. Drain off water and add onion, garlic, savory, olive oil and salt, and then mix.

Cheese

AHEAD OF TIME: Soak sunflower and pumpkin seeds overnight. Drain the water off and place seeds in a blender. To blender add vinegar oregano, onion, and salt--blend until smooth, adding water as needed.

Spread half the "cheese" (the sunflower/pumpkin blend) on the crust and spread until even. Arrange mushrooms over cheese then place vegetables and top with the remaining cheese. Or you can mix the mushrooms, vegetable with the cheese and spread over the crust.

Warm in a dehydrator at 100°F. for one to two hours if desired.

Olive Pizza

Makes 2-4 Servings

Ingredients

Crust

- 1 c. golden flax seed, ground in a coffee grinder
- 1 c. buckwheat, soaked
- 1 tbsp. Himalayan crystal salt
- 1-2 c. pure water
- ¼ c. raw coconut flour (optional)

Topping

- ½ c. sun dried olives
- ½ c. artichokes hearts (optional not a raw product)
- 1 c. nut mayo (page 71)

Sauce

- 1 c. dried tomatoes
- 1 tbsp. pizza seasoning
- 2 tbsp. olive oil
- 2 tsp. lemon powder

Directions

AHEAD OF TIME: Soak the buckwheat overnight, drain the water and rinse the buckwheat. Place the buckwheat in a food processor.

Blend together, tomatoes, pizza seasoning and olive oil in a blender.

Grind flax seeds in a coffee grinder and add to the food processor with buckwheat. Add salt and only enough water to make dough.

Roll the dough out into a circle, using the coconut flour to keep from sticking. This step could be done with ground flax seed as well.

Chop artichoke hearts. Place the sauce on the dough and layer on the artichoke hearts and olives. Top by dropping the mayo over the top, this becomes the cheese.

Warm at 100°F. in a dehydrator for an hour, or two.

Stuffing

Makes 6-8 Servings

Ingredients

- ½ c. dried onion
- ½ c. dried apple
- ¼ c. dried celery slices
- ¼ c. dried carrot
- ¼ c. raisins
- 1 c. pecans, soaked
- 1 c. almonds, soaked
- ½ c. golden flax seeds, ground
- 2 tbsp. cold pressed olive oil
- ¼ tsp. cayenne pepper
- ½ tsp. garlic powder
- ½ tsp. turmeric powder
- 1 tsp. Himalayan crystal salt
- pepper to taste

Directions

AHEAD OF TIME: Soak almonds and pecans overnight. Drain off water and place nuts in a food processor with ground flax combine until coarsely mixed. Add only enough water until it looks like thick dough. Place t nut mixture in a bowl.

Soak celery, onion, apple, and carrot, in water for 20 minutes. Drain off water and place the vegetables along with raisins, cayenne, garlic, turmeric, pepper, and salt in a food processor, pulse until very roughly chopped.

Gently mix in nut mixture. Place in a dish and dehydrate at 100°F. for about 8 hours or until desired moisture is achieved. Mix the stuffing about half way through the drying.

Basic Pate

Makes 4-6 Servings

Ingredients

- 2 c. favorite nut or seeds
- ½ tbsp. onion powder
- 2 tsp. dried parsley
- 1 tsp. garlic salt
- 1 tbsp. lemon powder
- ¼ c. water
- ¼ c. cold pressed olive oil
- Himalayan crystal salt to taste
- pepper to taste

Directions

AHEAD OF TIME: Soak preferred nut or seed overnight. Drain off water and place nuts in food processor add onion powder, garlic salt, lemon juice, olive oil, parsley, salt, and pepper combine until desired texture is achieved.

Use for dipping vegetables, on a salad--or as a filling. I stuff bell peppers with it.

Variation

Change the seasonings to any that you like. Examples of seasonings are; Mexican, Italian, Far East, French, Vegetable, and so forth; let your imagination be your guide.

Herbed Almond Spread

Makes 1 cup

Ingredients

- 1 c. almonds, soaked overnight
- 4 tbsp. lemon powder, made from grinding dried lemon
- 1 tbsp. cold pressed olive oil
- 1 tbsp. garlic powder
- ¼ tsp. Himalayan crystal salt
- 1 tsp. mustard powder
- ¼ c. dried parsley
- ½ c. water

Directions

AHEAD OF TIME: Soak the almonds overnight, drain off the water and peel the brown skin off.

Soak lemon powder in ¼ cup water for 20 minutes.

Place nuts, garlic, and salt in a food processor mix until it resembles a coarse meal. Add olive oil, garlic powder, salt, mustard powder, and parsley. Blend until it is a thick paste. Add water to thin- -as much as needed to achieve t smooth spread.

If no power is available use a hand food processor, or crush the nuts by hand in a mortar and pestle- -mix in the remaining ingredients.

Spread on crackers or use as a veggie dip.

Stroganoff

Makes 6-8 Servings

Ingredients

- 4 tbsp. dried shiitake mushrooms
- 4 tbsp. dried brown mushrooms
- ¼ c. cashews,
- ¼ tsp. Himalayan crystal salt
- 1 tsp. lemon powder
- 4 tbsp. water
- 1 tbsp. cold pressed olive oil
- 1 tbsp. sesame milk
- 2 tbsp. tahini
- 1 tbsp. poultry seasoning
- ½ c. dried onion
- ¼ tsp. paprika
- ½ tsp. thyme, dried
- 1 tbsp. dill, dried
- freshly ground pepper to taste
- pure water

Directions

Soak lemon powder in water for 20 minutes; this is now lemon juice. Soak mushroom for 20 minutes in lemon juice.

In a blender, combine mushrooms, cashews, salt, olive oil, lemon juice, sesame milk, tahini, poultry seasoning, onion, paprika, thyme, dill, and pepper adding water slowly to make it creamy.

Serve over shredded squash or sprouted wild rice.

Fun Fact

A single Portabella mushroom can contain more potassium than a banana.

Almond Butter

Makes 1 cup

Ingredients

- 1 c. raw almonds
- 4-5 tbsp. liquefied coconut or olive oil
- ½ tsp. Himalayan crystal salt (optional)

Directions

Place almonds in mortar and pestle. Grind into a fine powder and place in a bowl. This may need to be done in small amounts.

Once almond meal is in a bowl, use your hand to sift the large chunks of almond out of the bowl.

Using a pastry blender or fork, drizzle oil in one tablespoon at a time, until the desired constancy is achieved. You may need more or less oil to achieve the constancy you like.

Eclectic method: If you have a food processor, place dry almonds in the food processor and take the time necessary to get to a smooth constancy. If the almonds are too thick, add oil. (Water will make the mixture seized and ruin the almond butter).

Tahini

Makes 1 Cup

Ingredients

- ¾ c. sesame seeds
- 2 tbsp. cold pressed olive oil
- 1 tsp. Himalayan crystal salt
- 1 lemon, juiced
- ¼ c. water

Directions

Grind sesame seeds in a coffee grinder to make sesame flour. Soak lemon powder in water for 20 minutes this is lemon juice.

Place sesame flour in a bowl add salt and lemon juice mix. Gradually add oil until the desired consistency is achieved. It should be similar to peanut butter constancy.

Tahini Sauce

Makes 1 cup

Ingredients

- 2 tsp. onion salt
- ½ c. cold pressed olive oil
- 1 c. raw tahini
- 1 c. water
- 2-3 tbsp. garlic powder
- 2 tbsp. lemon powder
- dash of cumin
- Himalayan Crystal Salt to taste
- black pepper to taste
- 2 tbsp. parsley, dried

Directions

Place onion salt, tahini, olive oil, garlic powder, lemon powder, cumin, salt, black pepper and parsley in a blender mix until smooth.

Use tahini sauce as a dip or dressing. For dressing may want to thin a little.

Fruit Compote

Makes 4-6 Servings

Ingredients

- 2 tbsp. cinnamon, ground
- 1 tsp. vanilla
- 8 dried plums
- 8 dried figs
- 7 dried apricots
- ¼ c. dried cherries
- Himalayan crystal salt to taste
- black pepper to taste
- 2 tbsp. dried parsley

Directions

Soak fruit in water for at least 30 minutes.

In a blender mix 4 plums, 4 figs, 3 apricots and cherries--adding only enough fruit soaking water to blend.

In a bowl place remaining dried fruit, then pour the blender mixture over them. Add cinnamon and vanilla then chill for 3 hours.

Nut Yogurt

Makes 6-8 Servings

Ingredients

- 1 c. macadamia nuts or cashews
- 1 c. almond pulp, saved from making almond milk
- 1 tsp. vanilla
- 2 c. rejuvelac

Directions

Mix macadamia nuts, almond pulp, and vanilla in a blender--with rejuvelac. Mix until creamy. Chill for 3 hours.

Place the yogurt in bowls and top with compote or rehydrated fruit of your choice. Enjoy!

Note

Rejuvelac can be replaced with water and/or 2 tsp. probiotic powder to the blender.

Ricotta Cheese Sauce

Makes ½ cup

Ingredients

- 1c. cashews nuts
- ½ c. pumpkin seeds
- 1 tsp. garlic salt
- ½ tsp. Himalayan crystal salt
- ½ tsp. Italian seasoning
- ½ c. water or more as needed

Directions

AHEAD OF TIME: Soak pumpkin seeds overnight. Drain off the water and place seeds in a blender with cashews, Italian seasoning, garlic, and salt.

Purée until fluffy--using only enough water to run the blender. This should look a little bit like a cheese sauce.

Basic Seed Cheese

Makes 6-8 Servings

Ingredients

- 1 c. hulled raw sunflower seeds
- 1 c. hulled raw pumpkin seeds
- 1 c. rejuvelac

Directions

AHEAD OF TIME: Soak pumpkin and sunflower seeds overnight, drain off water.

Combine rejuvelac and seeds in a blender at high speed until it is a smooth thick paste-- about 4 minutes.

Pour the blender mixture into cheese cloth and place over a bowl or glass jar. Wrap the edges of the cloth and wrap, gently squeezing the liquid out. Hang the cloth ball over the bowl, and leave it for 8-12 hours.

Note:

The longer it stands the stronger the flavor will be. After the fermentation, discard any liquid that has settle in the bowl or jar. Store extra cheese in the refrigerator; covered tightly.

Tip

If you don't have rejuvelac, you can use lemon, vinegar and a cup of water instead. If you use this method, however, the fermentation time may need to be extended to 12 -18 hours.

After the fermentation time elapses, stick a spoon through the cheese on top and pour off and discard the liquid that has settled at the bottom of the jar. Store extra cheese in the refrigerator; cover tightly.

Vegan Feta Cheese

Makes 4-6 Servings

Ingredients

- 1 c. almonds, soaked overnight
- ¼ c. fresh basil or thyme, oregano or other spice you choose
- ¼ tsp. Himalayan crystal salt
- ½ c. rejuvalic

Directions

AHEAD OF TIME: Soak almonds overnight and then drain the water off. While wet peel the brown skin off the almonds.

Into a blender place rejuvelac, almonds and salt. Blend at high speed, until it is a smooth.

Chop fresh or add dried basil and pulse in a blender --or mix by hand. Make sure it is gently pulsed-- otherwise you will have a green cheese.

Pour blender mixture into cheese cloth and place over a bowl or glass jar. Wrap the edges of the cloth and wrap, gently squeezing the liquid out. Hang the cloth ball over the bowl, and leave it for 8-12 hours.

After the fermentation, discard any liquid that has settle in the bowl or jar. Store extra cheese in the refrigerator; covered tightly.

Note:

The longer it stands the stronger the flavor will be.

Tip

If you don't have Rejuvelac, you can use lemon, vinegar and a cup of water instead. If you use this method, however, the fermentation time may need to be extended to 12 -18 hours.

Rawmesan

Makes 1 cup

Ingredients

- ½ c. cashews
- ¼ c. raw, pumpkin seeds
- ½ tsp. Himalayan crystal salt
- ½ tsp. dried dill
- ½ tsp. nutritional yeast (optional)

Directions

In a food processor, grind cashews and pumpkin seed into a powder. Add salt and dill--pulse a few more times.

Nacho Cheese

Makes ½ cup

Ingredients

- 1 c. basic seed cheese
- 3 dried Anaheim peppers
- 1 tsp garlic powder
- 1 tbsp. onion powder
- 1 c. dried tomatoes
- 2 dried red bell peppers
- 1 tsp. lemon powder
- 1 ½ tsp. Himalayan crystal salt

Directions

AHEAD OF TIME: Make basic seed cheese.

In a mortar and pestle crush dried Anaheim peppers, tomatoes, and bell peppers then place in bowl. Add basic seed cheese, garlic powder, onion powder, salt, and lemon powder and mix well. If mixture is too thick adding rejuvelac or water.

Herbed Vegan Cream Cheese

Makes ½ cup

Ingredients

- ½ c. cashews
- ½ c. pumpkin seeds, soaked
- 2 tsp. lemon powder
- 5 tbsp. water
- ½ tsp. Himalayan crystal salt
- ¼ tsp. nutritional yeast (optional)
- ½ tsp. dried oregano
- ½ tsp. dried parsley
- ½ tsp. dried basil
- ¼ tsp. dried dill

Directions

AHEAD OF TIME: Soak pumpkin seeds overnight. Drain off water and add place seeds in food processor.

To food processor, add cashews, lemon juice, salt, nutritional yeast, oregano, parsley, basil, and dill--blend until smooth. Add a tablespoon at a time of water to thin the mixture if needed.

Make lemon juice by soaking the lemon powder in water for 20 minutes.

Place in a dish and cover. Chill for about an hour or until ready to serve. Can store in a sealed container for 4-7 days.

Sour Cream

Makes 4-6 Servings

Ingredients

- 1 c. almonds, soaked
- 1tsp. lemon powder
- 1 tbsp. raw apple cider vinegar
- ½ c. pure water as needed
- Himalayan crystal salt to taste

Directions

AHEAD OF TIME: Soak almonds overnight, then drain off the water. While almonds are wet, peel off the brown skin.

In a blender, puree almonds, lemon powder, vinegar, and salt and blend until creamy--add water as needed.

Note

If no power is available, grind dry nuts to a powder and then add the remaining ingredients, mixing until smooth and creamy.

Spicy Cheese

Makes 4-6 Servings

Ingredients

- 2 c. almonds, soaked overnight
- ½ c. water
- 2 tbsp. lemon powder
- ½ tsp. Himalayan crystal salt
- 1 tsp. dill
- ¼ c onion powder
- 1 dried red bell pepper, diced
- 3 tbsp. chili powder
- ½ c. dried tomatoes,

Directions

AHEAD of TIME: Soak almonds in water overnight-- then drain off the water.

Make lemon juice by soaking the lemon powder in water for 20 minutes. Soak tomatoes and bell peppers in water for 30 minutes.

Place almonds in a food processor and chop until fine. Add tomatoes, bell peppers, lemon juice, spices, and chill.

If no power is available, use a hand food processor or use a mortar and pastel and finely grind almonds. Finely chop the remaining ingredients and mix by hand.

Serve on flax crackers, other raw crackers, or with veggies as a dip.

Fun Fact

A German immigrant in New Braunfel, Texas is created with the creations of the first commercial blend of chili Powder in 1882.

Nut Mayo

Makes 2 cups

Ingredients

- 2 c. cashews or soaked and peeled almonds
- 3 tbsp. onion powder
- ½ c. cold pressed olive oil
- ¾ c. water
- 1-2 tbsp. Himalayan crystal salt
- 2 tbsp. raw apple cider vinegar
- water as needed.

Directions

Blend nuts, onion powered, olive oil, salt, and vinegar until smooth--adding water as needed.

If no power, powder dry nuts with a mortar and pestle. Then add the other ingredients mixing well, adding water until a smooth texture is achieved.

Basic Flax Crackers

Makes 6-8 Servings

Ingredients

- 1c. flaxseeds
- ¾ c. pure water
- ¼ tsp. Himalayan crystal salt

Directions

Soak flaxseed in the water with the salt for about 15 minutes--or until it becomes thick but not too stiff.

Evenly spread the mixture on a nonstick dehydrator sheet. Dry for about 6 hours. Take the crackers out and flip them--pull off the nonstick dehydrator sheet.

Continue drying for another 6-12 hours or until the crackers are dry.

Notes

There are many ways to make flax crackers. If you do not like whole flaxseed, before you add water, grind them in a coffee grinder before adding the water.

Mix up flavors by changing the spices and adding vegetables, such as corn for corn flax crackers, or nuts and seed such as buckwheat, pumpkin seed, sunflower seeds and so forth.

Example: For Italian flaxseed crackers, add Italian spices and tomatoes. Make sure to chop the tomatoes well.

Use your imagination and make the flax crackers you enjoy.

Pizza Crackers

Makes 4-6 Servings

Ingredients

- 1 c. almonds, soaked overnight
- ½ c. pumpkin seeds
- ½ c. dried red bell pepper
- ½ c. carrots, dried, shredded
- ½ c. dried celery
- ¼ c. dried onion, chopped
- 1 tsp. parsley
- ½ c. raw tahini
- 1 tsp. garlic powder
- 1 tsp. dried basil
- 3 tbsp. pizza seasoning
- 1 tsp. onion powder
- 1 tbsp. Himalayan crystal salt
- 1 tsp. cold pressed olive oil
- pure water as needed

Directions

AHEAD of TIME: Soak almonds and pumpkin seeds overnight, drain the water off.

Soak the dried bell pepper, celery, carrots, and onion for about 30 minutes, drain off water-- but save this water.

Place almonds, pumpkin seeds, bell pepper, celery, carrots, parsley, garlic, olive oil, tahini, and spices in the food processor and combine until mixed. Add only enough of the saved vegetable soaking water as needed to combine the ingredients.

Spread cracker mix about a half an inch thick on a nonstick dehydrator sheet. Lightly cut into desired shapes. Dehydrate at 100°F for about 3 hours.

Flip and carefully remove the nonstick dehydrator sheet. Continue drying on the rack in the dehydrator until dry--approximately 4 more hours.

Veggie Crackers

Makes 4-6 Servings

Ingredients

- 1-2 cloves garlic
- ½ c. tomato
- 1 c. carrots, shredded
- 1 c. raw sunflower seeds, soaked
- 1 c. raw pumpkin seeds, soaked
- ½ c. red bell pepper, finely chopped
- ½ c. onion, finely chopped
- ½ c. celery stalks, chopped
- 1 tsp. caraway seeds
- 1 tsp. Himalayan crystal salt
- 2 tbsp. cold pressed olive oil
- 3 tbsp. raw tahini

Directions

AHEAD of TIME: Soak pumpkin and sunflower seeds overnight. Drain water off.

Rehydrate carrots, tomatoes, bell peppers, and celery in water for about 30 minutes. Drain off the water and save it to use if needed for further mixing.

Combine seeds and carrots in the food processor until finely chopped add tomato, garlic, bell pepper, onion, celery, tahini, olive oil, and salt--Blend until everything well incorporated. Add vegetable soaking water if too thick.

Spread the cracker mix onto a nonstick dehydrator sheet--a quarter of an inch thick. Lightly score the crackers into squares or the shapes desired, and place in a dehydrator at 100°F for about 4 hours. Flip the crackers and carefully remove the nonstick dehydrator sheet. Continue drying cracker until the desired crispness is obtained.

Sesame Crackers

Makes 6-8 Servings

Ingredients

- 1 tbsp. lemon powder
- ¼ lemon, juiced
- 1 tsp. cumin
- 1 tsp. curry powder
- 1 c. sunflower seeds
- 1 c. sesame seeds
- 1 c. dried carrots
- 4 tbsp. onion powder
- 1 tsp. raw tahini

Directions

AHEAD of TIME: Soak sesame and sunflower seeds separately, overnight. Drain off water, and carefully rinse the seeds--set them aside.

Soak lemon powder in water for about 20 minutes for lemon juice.

In a food processor, combine ¾ cup sesame seeds, all the sunflower seeds, and add the lemon juice, curry powder, dried carrot pieces, onion powder, and raw tahini--mix until well combined.

Form dough into balls using 2 teaspoons of batter. Place the dough balls on nonstick dehydrator sheet and flatten to a quarter of an inch thick. Sprinkle with remaining sesame seeds.

Dehydrate at 105°F for 2 hours. Flip the crackers and carefully remove nonstick dehydrator sheet. Continue dehydrating for 4 or more hours until desired crispness is obtained.

Lemon Poppy Muffins

Makes 4-6 Servings

Ingredients

- 1 c. cashews
- 1 c. almond pulp
- 3 tbsp. lemon powder
- 1 c. dates
- 1 tbsp. poppy seeds
- 1 tsp. Himalayan crystal salt
- water as needed

Directions

AHEAD OF TIME: Soak almonds overnight then drain off the water. While still wet peel off the brown skin. Note: if desired use almond pulp leftover from making almond milk.

In a food processor, combine almonds, cashews, lemon powder, and dates until well mixed. Add water if needed to help dough stick together. Stir in poppy seeds and salt until well combined.

Make a ball out of 2 tablespoon dough and place on nonstick dehydrator sheet. Continue until all the dough is used.

Place in dehydrator at 105° F. for about 4-6 hours. Flip the muffins and carefully remove the nonstick dehydrator sheet and continue drying another 4-6 hours or until desired moisture is obtained. Enjoy!

Note

If dates are hard soak in enough water to cover. Use the soaking water to mix in the dough.

Cranberry Muffins

Makes 6-8 Servings

Ingredients

- 2 c. almond pulp, from making milk
- 1 ½ c. dried cranberry
- ½ c. freeze dried pineapple
- 1 c. dried apples, chopped
- 1 c. dates
- 1 tbsp. cinnamon, ground
- 1 tsp. cloves, ground
- 1 tsp. nutmeg, ground

Directions

After removing the pits from the dates, soak them in just enough water to cover with pineapple and apples for about 20 minutes.

Set the soaking water aside and use this liquid to achieve the desired texture.

In a food processor, combine almond pulp and 1 cup cranberries until coarsely chopped. Add remaining cranberries, pineapple, and spice until mixed.

Drop the dough with a spoon or scoop onto a dehydrator tray covered with a nonstick sheet, forming muffins.

Hint:

The thicker they are, the longer they will take to dry and the more "muffin like" they will be. Thinner ones will dry quicker and be more like cookies--if they are too thick, they will start fermenting.

Dehydrate at 105°F. for 4-6 hours, then turn the muffins. Remove nonstick sheet and continue drying for another 4-6 hours or until the desired moisture is obtained.

Tip

To mix with no power, chop soaked cranberries, pineapple and apples--mix in with the almond pulp or crushed almonds along with spices and combine all ingredients by hand.

Use a sun dryer, and make sure the muffins are thin so they will not ferment. You can eat them without drying as an option.

Fun Facts

Native American medicine men used cranberries in poultices to draw poison form arrow wounds.

Contrary to popular belief, cranberries do not grow in water. They are grown on sandy bogs or marshes. Because cranberries float, some bogs are flooded when the fruit is ready for harvesting.

Apple Carrot Muffins

Makes 4-6 Servings

Ingredients

- 1 c. buckwheat, sprouted
- 1 c. almond pulp, left over from making milk
- ½ c. dried carrot
- ¾ c. dates
- 1 c. raisins
- ½ c. apples,
- ½ c. walnuts, chopped
- 1 tbsp. cinnamon
- 1 tsp. cardamom
- 1 tsp. cloves

Directions

AHEAD of TIME: Make fresh almond milk or use the saved almond pulp from early milk making. Soak buckwheat and walnuts overnight in separate bowls.

Soak dried apples and carrots in water for 20 minutes.

Using a food processor, mix buckwheat, almond pulp, walnuts, and dates until well mixed. Move buckwheat mixture to a bowl, add raisins, apple, and spice, mix by hand until everything is well combined.

Drop dough onto nonstick dehydrator sheet using a spoon or scoop; place into the dehydrator at 105°F. for about 4 to 6 hours. Flip the muffins and carefully remove the nonstick dehydrator sheet. Continue drying another 4 to 6 hours until the desired moisture is obtained.

Nancy's Bread

Makes 6-8 Servings

Ingredients

- 1 c. gold flax, ground
- 2 c. buckwheat, sprouted
- 2 tsp. Himalayan crystal salt
- 1 c. dry buckwheat, ground
- ¼ c. raw coconut flour

Directions

Soak 1 cup buckwheat overnight, and drain water off. In a food processor, combine soaked buckwheat, ground flax, and salt. Mix until a thick dough.

Using a coffee grinder, grind dry buckwheat--this becomes buckwheat flour. Use buckwheat flour to thicken the dough if it is too sticky in the food processor.

Sprinkle coconut flour on the counter and knead the dough until soft and pliable. If the dough is too sticky, add more coconut flour.

Shape dough and place on dehydrator tray and dry for about 1 hour at 100°F.

Notes

You may use buckwheat flour instead of coconut. The coconut flour helps the bread to be lighter.

The bread works better if made on a warm day or in a warm place.

Corn Bread

Makes 6-8 Servings

Ingredients

- 2 c. almonds, soaked overnight
- ½ c. cashews
- ½ c. walnuts, soaked overnight
- 1 c. golden flax seed, ground
- 2 c. dried corn
- ¼ c. raw liquid sweetener
- 2 tsp. Himalayan crystal salt
- 1 tsp. garlic salt
- pure water as needed

Directions

AHEAD OF TIME: Soak almonds and walnuts overnight, drain off water.

Place almonds and cashews into a food processor and blend adding fresh water as needed until it looks like dough. Place in a bowl and set aside.

Soak dried corn in pure water for about 20 minutes; drain off the water but save it to be used in the food processor --as needed.

In a food processor add corn, walnuts, garlic, salt, and raw sweetener. Combine until well mixed, adding water as needed to achieve semi-creamy state. Place in the same bowl with the almond and cashew mixture--gently mix by hand.

Grind golden flaxseed in a coffee grinder. Slowly add ground flax into the bowl and combine very well. Let it sit for 5 to 10 minutes.

Put corn bread a nonstick dehydrator sheet over the tray for stabilization and spread about ¼ of an inch thick. Then score it lightly with a pizza cutter or knife into rectangles pieces.

Dry at 105°F for about 3 hours flipping it halfway through, removing the nonstick dehydrator sheet and setting it back onto the tray. Continue drying for approximately 3 more hours. The bread is done when it still moist and easy to lift. Serve with raw honey butter.

Tip:

A pizza cutter is a great way to score crackers, just be careful not to press too hard into the dehydrator sheet.

Honey Butter

Makes ½ cup

Ingredients

- ½ c. coconut oil
- 4 tbsp. raw honey
- ¼ tsp. turmeric
- 1 tsp. Himalayan crystal salt

Directions

Mix Coconut oil, honey, turmeric, and salt. by hand into fluffy well-mixed.

Garlic Bread

Makes 6-8 Servings

Ingredients

Bread

- 1 c. gold flax, ground
- 1 ½ c. buckwheat
- ½ c. almonds, soaked
- 2 tsp. Himalayan crystal salt
- ¼ c. raw coconut flour

'Garlic Butter'

- ½ c. coconut oil
- ¼ c. rawmesan (page 103)
- ½ tsp. garlic powder
- pinch of basil leaves

Directions

AHEAD OF TIME: Soak ½-cup buckwheat and almonds overnight in separate bowls--drain water off.

In a food processor combine buckwheat, almonds, ground flax, and salt. Mix until a thick dough.

Using a coffee grinder, grind dry buckwheat. This becomes buckwheat flour. Use the buckwheat flour to thicken the dough if it is too sticky in the food processor. Form dough into round circles.

Sprinkle coconut flour on counter and knead dough until soft and pliable. If dough is too sticky, add more coconut or buckwheat flour.

Shape bread into slices or sticks and place on dehydrator tray. Brush with garlic butter and dry for about 1 hour at 100°F.

To make the garlic butter combine coconut oil, rawmesan, garlic powder, and basil in a small bowl--mix with a spoon until well combined.

Fun Fact

It's believed that Egyptian pharaohs plied their pyramid builders with garlic for strength.

Raw Bagels

Makes 4-6 Servings

Ingredients

- 1 c. buckwheat, ground
- ½ c. raw coconut four
- ½ c. flaxseeds, ground
- 1 c. walnuts, ground
- 2 tbsp. chia seeds
- 1 clove garlic
- 2 tbsp. onion
- 2 tbsp. coconut nectar
- 1 lemon, juiced
- 1 c. water
- ¼ c. cashews
- 2 tbsp. nutritional yeast (optional)

Directions

Place dry walnuts in a food processor and mix until flour is formed. Grind flaxseeds and buckwheat in a coffee grinder and add to the food processor, along with chia seeds and set aside.

In a blender, place garlic, onion, coconut nectar, lemon juice, water, cashews, and nutritional yeast--mix until creamy.

Add blender ingredients to the dry ingredients into the food processor, mix until a dough is formed.

Sprinkle coconut flour onto a clean surface and knead dough then let the dough rest for 10-20 minutes.

Use about ¼ cup size of dough for each bagel and form into a ball. Flatten balls and make a hole in the middle with your finger. Place on a dehydrator and dry for about 2 hours. Cut each bagel horizontally in half and continue drying for another 2 or so hours. It is ready when the desired texture is achieved.

Carob 'Ice Cream'

Makes 6-8 Servings

Ingredients

- 1 c. cashews
- 1 ½ c. water
- ¼ c. dried stevia leaves or other raw sweetener
- 1 tsp. Himalayan crystal salt
- ½ c. carob powder

Directions

Place all the ingredients into a blender and combine until smooth.

Using cheesecloth over a container strain out all the large particles. This creates a very smooth base.

Pour mixture into the ice cream maker and follow manufacture instructions. It should reach ideal consistency in about 20 minutes.

Option: If you don't have an ice cream maker, you can place ½ cup of the base into a plastic sealable bag and tightly seal it. Put ice and salt into a gallon storage container with a lid. Place the sandwich bag in with the salt and ice. Then shake the entire container until the mixture is frozen and resembles ice cream--about 5-10 minutes.

Remove the ice cream bag and serve in small bowls. Enjoy!

Strawberry 'Ice Cream'

Makes 6-8 Servings

Ingredients

- 1 c. cashews
- ½ c. raisins
- 1 ½ c. water
- ¼ c. coconut nectar
- 1 tsp. raw vanilla powder or 1 tbsp. vanilla extract
- 1 tbsp. coconut oil
- ½ c. freeze-dried strawberries

Directions

Place freeze-dried strawberries, raisins, coconut nectar, vanilla, coconut oil, and cashews into a blender and combine until smooth. Use raisin water if needed.

With cheesecloth placed over a container, strain out all the large particles and create a very smooth base.

Pour mixture into the ice cream maker and follow manufacture instructions. It should reach ideal consistency in about 20 minutes.

Option: If you don't have an ice cream maker, you can place ½ cup of the base into a plastic sealable bag and tightly seal it. Put the ice and salt into a gallon storage container with a lid. Place the sandwich bag in with the salt and ice. Then shake the entire container until the mixture is frozen and resembles ice cream--about 5-10 minutes.

Remove the ice cream bag and serve in small bowls. Enjoy!

Basil 'Ice Cream'

Makes 6-8 Servings

Ingredients

- 1 c. cashews
- 1 ½ c. water
- ½ c. lemon, juiced
- ¼ c. dried stevia leaves
- 1 tsp. Himalayan crystal salt
- 3 tbsp. dried basil leaves (or mint leaves)

Directions

Place cashews, stevia, basil, salt, lemon, and water into a blender and combine until smooth.

Strain out all the large particles, using cheesecloth stretched over a container for a very smooth base.

Pour this creamy mixture into the ice cream maker and follow manufacture instructions. It should reach ideal consistency in about 20 minutes.

Option: If you don't have an ice cream maker, you can place ½ cup of the base into a sandwich-size sealable plastic bag and tightly seal. Place ice and salt into a gallon storage container with a lid.

Place the bagged ice cream mixture into the salt and ice. Then shake the container until the mixture is frozen and resemble ice cream, about 5-10 minutes.

Remove the ice cream bag and place it into small bowls.

Cream Frosting

Makes 6-8 Servings

Ingredients

- 1 c. macadamia nuts or cashews
- ½ c. raw coconut oil
- ½ c. raw liquid sweetener
- ¼ - ¾ c. water

Directions

In a blender, combine nuts, coconut oil, and liquid sweetener, until creamy, adding only enough water until desired thickness is achieved.

Note

This can be done by hand with a pestle or hand blender if no power is available.

Soft Gingerbread Cookies

Makes 6-8 Servings

Ingredients

- 1 c. dates
- 1 c. buckwheat
- ½ c. flax seed
- ½ tsp. allspice
- 1 tsp. cinnamon, ground
- ¾ tsp. cardamom, ground
- ¼ tsp. Himalayan crystal salt
- ½ tsp. clove, ground
- ½ c. coconut nectar
- 2 tsp. ginger, ground
- ½ c. raw coconut flour
- cream frosting (page 121, optional)

Directions

AHEAD OF TIME: Soak buckwheat overnight. Drain off water.

Place dates in a food processor and mix, add soaked buckwheat continue mixing until well combined.

Grind flax seed in a coffee grinder then adds to the food processor with the buckwheat. Add allspice, cinnamon, cardamom, salt, clove, ginger, and coconut nectar mix until well combined.

Incorporate coconut flour, or buckwheat flour made from dried ground buckwheat; sprinkle some coconut flour on the counter. Knead the dough from the food processor, adding more coconut flour until dough is firm and looks like cookie dough.

Roll dough out to about ¼ inch thick and using a cookie cutter, cut cookies. Place on a nonstick dehydrator sheet and dry for about 2 hours. Flip and remove the nonstick sheet and continue drying for another 2-4 hours to the desired texture. After drying, make the cream frosting, and decorate the cookies.

Note

May eat before drying or dry in the sun.

Becky's Cheesecake

Makes 6-8 Servings

Ingredients

Crust
- 1 c. pecans or walnuts, soaked

Filling
- 2 c. cashews
- 2 tbsp. lime powder
- ½ c. raw liquid sweetener
- dash of Himalayan crystal salt
- ½ - 2 c. water as needed
- 1 tsp. vanilla extract

Directions

AHEAD OF TIME: Soak pecans or walnuts overnight. Drain off the water.

In a food processor, combine dates and pecans until finely chopped. Press the mix into a pie plate for crust, and set aside.

In a blender, combine cashews, lime powder, sweetener, salt, vanilla, and water until smooth and creamy, using only enough water to achieve a very thick and smooth texture.

Pour the thick filling into the pecan/date crust--chill for several hours before serving. Top with any seasonal fruit or jelly if desired.

Variation

For Chocolate Chip Cheesecake add ¼ c. raw carob powder, ½ c. raw cacao nibs, and ½ c. cocoa butter to the filling.

Brownies

Makes 6-8 Servings

Ingredients

- 1 ½ c. dried carrots
- 3 c. walnuts, soaked
- 2 c. cashews
- 2 c. dates
- ½ tsp. Himalayan crystal salt
- 2 tsp. cinnamon
- 1 c. raw carob powder
- ¼ c. coconut oil
- 1 tsp. pure vanilla extract

Directions

AHEAD OF TIME: Soak walnuts overnight--drain water off.

Place soaked nuts into a food processor with carrots, cashews, salt, cinnamon, carob, oil, vanilla, and dates--combine until well mixed.

Put the mix onto a nonstick dehydrator sheet tray and shape it into a square, an inch thick on the tray. Dehydrate brownies approximately four hours, and then flip them directly onto the tray, pulling off the nonstick dehydrator sheet. Continue to dry for another 4-hours.

Serve with Carob Frosting (page 127) or Cream Frosting (page 121).

Celebration Cake

Makes 6-8 Servings

Ingredients

Cake

- 5 c. pecans, soaked
- 3 c. dates
- 1 c. raw carob powder
- ½ tsp. Himalayan crystal salt
- 1 c. buckwheat, ground

Berry Syrup

- ½ c. favorite dried berries
- water

Carob Icing

- 1 c. cashews
- ¾ c. water
- 1 tbsp. vanilla extract
- 5 tbsp. raw carob powder

Directions

AHEAD of TIME: Soak pecans overnight, drain off the water.

Soak dates in enough water to cover for 30 minutes.

Grind the dry buckwheat in a coffee grinder.

In a food processor, combine nuts and dates until smooth. Add carob, salt, and the ground buckwheat.

Divide the cake "batter" into three equal parts, form into rounds, making sure they are about the same size, and set them aside.

NOTE: The batter will be thick and should hold be easy to shape.

Powder dried berries in a blender, add water and mix until well combined. Make it thin enough to brush onto the cake.

Using a blender, combine cashews, water, vanilla, and carob until fluffy. Use this frosting and berry sauce on each layer to create all three layers.

Fun Facts

One of the first wedding cakes wasn't actually cake at all, it was bread that had eggs and butter added and sweetened with honey. In ancient Rome, bread was broken over the bride's head to symbolize good fortune and fertility to the couple.

During the 17th century, in England, people believed that keeping fruitcakes under the pillow of those who are unmarried will give them sweet dreams about their fiancée.

The first birthday cake was originally a cake given as an offering on a person's birthday. Some believe that the tradition of birthday candles began in Ancient Greece, when people brought cakes adorned with lit candles to the temple of Artemis, goddess of the hunt. Others believe that the tradition of birthday candles started with the Germans in 1700s.

Black Bottom Coconut Bar

Makes 8-10 Servings

Ingredients

Black Bottom

- 1 c. unrefined coconut oil
- ¾ c. raw coconut nectar
- 1 c. raw carob powder
- 2 tbsp. pure vanilla
- 2 c. walnuts or pecans

Coconut Topping

- 2 c. macadamia nuts
- ¾ c. coconuts oil
- 1 tsp. turmeric
- 2 c. coconut, shredded
- 2 tsp. pure vanilla extract

Directions

In a food processor, chop dried walnuts until finely chopped.

Melt coconut oil in a bowl over a warm pan of hot water or double broiler, keeping the temperature of the oil about 100°F.

To coconut oil, add coconut nectar, carob powder, and vanilla stir until it starts to get thick. Then add chopped nuts to the mix. Press it into the bottom of a large cake pan. Cover and set it aside.

In a clean food processor, mix macadamia nuts, coconut oil, turmeric, shredded coconut, and vanilla mix until very well combined and almost creamy.

Spread coconut mixture over the top of carob black bottom mixture. Place in refrigerator until hard. Cut into bars and enjoy eating.

Cinnamon Rolls Pizza

Makes 6-8 Servings

Ingredients

Crust:

- 2 c. almond pulp, left from making almond milk
- 1 c. dates, pitted and soaked

Cinnamon Topping:

- ½ c. walnuts or pecans, soaked
- 1 ½ tbsp. cinnamon, ground
- 1 c. raisins
- ½ c. raw coconut sugar
- 2 tbsp. cold pressed olive oil
- ½ tsp. turmeric
- 1 tsp. Himalayan crystal salt
- ½ inch vanilla bean or ½ tbsp. vanilla extract

Creamy Glaze:

- ½ c. macadamia nut
- ½ c. cashews
- ½ c. raw coconut nectar
- 1 lemon, juiced
- ½ tbsp. coconut oil
- water as needed

Directions

Crust

Soak dates in water for about 20 minutes, save soaking water for later use. In a food processor, combine almond pulp and dates until well mixed. Add date water as needed. Form dough into a round, about ¼ - ½ thick, and place in dehydrator for about 2 hours at 100°F.

Cinnamon Topping

In a small container, mix olive oil, turmeric, and salt then brush over crust. In a food processor, coarsely chop walnuts or pecans then place in a bowl. To the bowl add cinnamon, raisins, vanilla, and coconut sugar then mix well. Evenly spread mixture over the crust pressing down to push topping into crust. Place in dehydrator for about 2 more hours at 100°F.

Creamy Glaze

Soak cashews and macadamia nuts for 10 minutes. Drain off water and place nuts into a blender. To the blender add lemon juice, coconut nectar, and coconut oil then blend until a smooth and creamy adding water as needed to achieve the desired texture. Drizzle glaze over the pizza before serving.

Peanut Butter Bars

Makes 6-8 Servings

Ingredients

- 2 c. walnuts
- 2 c. oat groats, ground in
- ½ c. raw tahini
- ½ c. raw almond butter
- 3 tbsp. cold pressed olive oil
- 1 tsp. Himalayan crystal salt
- 1 tsp. turmeric
- ¾ c. raw liquid sweetener
- 1 tbsp. pure vanilla

Peanut Butter

- ½ c. raw tahini
- ½ c. raw almond butter
- ¼ c. raw liquid sweetener

Carob Frosting

- 3 tbsp. raw liquid sweetener
- ¾ c. raw carob powder
- 2 tsp. pure water

Directions

Make sure the nuts are dry, if they are not, the texture will be wrong.

Grind oat groats in a coffee grinder and place in a food processor add walnuts, tahini, almond butter, olive oil, salt, turmeric, and sweetener in the food processor and mix until it looks like cookie dough. Dehydrate at 100°F. for about 8 hours and place in the refrigerator for 5 hours.

Peanut Butter

In a bowl, mix tahini, almond butter, and sweetener to form 'peanut butter' by hand until smooth. Spread the 'peanut butter' on the bars.

Carob Frosting

Place carob in a small bowl, add sweetener, and mix slowly adding the water; you may need more or less. You are looking for a creamy frosting. Spread on top of the peanut butter.

Fudge

Makes 4-6 Servings

Ingredients

- 1 c. unrefined raw coconut oil
- ¾ c. raw coconut butter
- 1 c. raw liquid sweetener
- 1 c. raw carob powder
- 2 tbsp. pure vanilla
- 2 c. walnuts or pecans (optional)

Directions

Melt coconut oil in a warm pan or a double boiler over hot water--make sure the internal temperature of the coconut oil does not go above 100°F.

Add coconut nectar or raw honey, carob, and the vanilla-- mix all until it's smooth and starts to thicken. Add pecans and pour into a cake pan.

Cover and refrigerate for at least an hour. To serve: Cut into pieces and keep any leftovers in the refrigerator. It will melt if left in the warm.

Blond Ambition

Makes 6-8 Servings

Ingredients

- 1 ½ c. sesame seeds, do not soak
- ¾ c. unsweetened shredded coconut
- ½ c. raw tahini
- ¼ c. raw almond butter
- ½ - ¾ c. raw liquid sweetener

Directions

Combine tahini, almond butter, and sweetener in a bowl. Slowly add sesame seeds and shredded coconut--mix well.

Spread the mixture into a pan, smoothing with a spatula, or using a small scoop and making balls. Refrigerate until firm--about 2 hours. Enjoy!

Crumb Cake

Makes 6-8 Servings

Ingredients

Cake

- 3 ½ c. pecans
- 1 ½ c. oat groats, grinder
- 1 c. dates, pitted
- 1 tbsp. cinnamon

Filling

- 2 c. dates, pitted
- 1 c. water
- 3 tbsp. orange powder
- 1 tsp. vanilla extract

Directions

Rehydrate orange powder in one-cup water. Soak the two-cups of pitted dates with the orange powder and water 30-60 minutes.

CAKE: In a food processor, pulse pecans and add one-cup pitted dates and chop together.

In a coffee grinder, finely grind oat groats. Add them into the food processor with the nuts and date mix, as well as the sweetener and cinnamon—combine well.

Scoop out half of the cake mixture and press it firmly into a pan. Set aside the remaining half of the cake mixture for later use.

FILLING: In a clean food processor, combine the PRE-soaked dates and orange juice with vanilla until smooth. Evenly pour the filling over the cake in the pan. Using the other half of the cake mixture, crumble it evenly across the top. Dehydrate at 105°F for about 2 hours.

Note

Make orange powder by drying oranges in slices. Powder them in a coffee grinder or food processor. To rehydrate, add water to the powder until the desired flavor.

Coconut Sugar Bumps

Makes 4-6 Servings

Ingredients

- ¾ c. flaked oat groats (optional: old-fashioned oatmeal)
- ½ c. raw coconut sugar
- 1 ¾ c. raw almond butter

Directions

In a bowl combine oats, almond butter, coconut sugar, and shredded coconut until well mixed. Roll the mixture into ½-inch balls and then roll in coconut sugar.

Raspberry Lemon Cake

Makes 6-8 Servings

Ingredients

Cake

- 1 ½ c. cashews
- 1 ½ c. pecans, soaked
- ¼ c. raw liquid sweetener
- 2 tsp. lemon powder
- 1 tsp. vanilla extract
- ½ tsp. nutmeg
- 1 tbsp. poppy seeds

Raspberry Frosting

- 1 ½ c. macadamia nuts or cashews
- ¼ c. water
- 1 tbsp. lemon powder
- ¼ c. raw liquid sweetener
- 1 c. freeze dried raspberries
- 1 tsp. vanilla extract

Topping

- ½ c. freeze dried raspberries
- 2 tbsp. poppy seeds

Directions

For lemon juice soak, powdered lemon in a cup water or about 20 minutes mix until well mixed. Use ¾ cup for cake and ¼ for frosting.

Cake

In food processor--combine macadamia nuts, pecans, raw sweetener, lemon juice, vanilla, and nutmeg--and mix well. If the cake is not firm enough, add some slippery elm or coconut to thicken.

Form cake and place on a nonstick dehydrator sheet and dry at 100°F. for about 3 hours. Flip it about halfway through, removing nonstick dehydrator sheet and carefully placing it back on the dehydrator tray.

NOTE: If it's going to be a layered cake, form shapes of equal size.

Raspberry Frosting

In a blender, combine cashews, raw sweetener, lemon juice, raspberries, and vanilla --blend until creamy and light.

Frost the cake with the raspberry frosting. For a layered cake, put some frosting in between the layers.

To decorate, sprinkle with poppy seeds and powdered freeze-dried raspberries.

Fun Fact

A mixture composed of an equal amount of warm water and lemon juice is used as a homemade remedy for a sore throat gargle. Lemon juice has excellent antibacterial properties, as well as vitamin C.

Lemon Pie

Makes 6-8 Servings

Ingredients

- 1 ½ c. pecans
- 1 c. dates
- 1 ½ c. water
- ½ c. lemon powder
- 5 c. golden raisins (soaked)

Directions

In a bowl, soak five cups of golden raisins with the lemon powder and water for 30 minutes.

Use a food processor to mix and blend the pecans well and pitted dates. Press the mix into a pie plate for the crust and set aside.

In a blender, combine the raisins and lemon until well mixed. Use soaking raisin soaking water as needed to reach a creamy smooth texture. Pour into the pie plate and refrigerate.

OPTION: Top with a Cashew Cream topping (page 133)

Yummy Oatmeal Cookies

Makes 6-8 Servings

Ingredients

- 2 c. walnuts
- 2 c. oat groats, flaked
- 1 c. coconut sugar
- 1 c. dates
- ½ c. almond butter
- 1 tsp. Himalayan crystal salt
- 2 tsp. coconut oil
- 1 tsp. turmeric

Directions

Soak pitted dates in water for about 30 minutes. Take the dates out of the soaking liquid and place them in the food processor.

In food processor, place walnuts and oat flakes. Add coconut sugar, almond butter, salt, coconut oil, and turmeric combine until well mixed.

Form dough into round cookies, place it on a nonstick dehydrator sheet, and then put them in the dehydrator for about 4 hours. Flip cookies and remove the dehydrator sheet. Continue to dry for about 3 more hours or until desired dryness is achieved.

Note

To make oat flakes-- Use a pasta maker to press the rinsed, soaked overnight and drained oat groats to make "oat flakes" and then dehydrate to use--or store. There are grain flakers on the market to make grain flakes (such as Bosch). Or--replace the oat groats with old-fashioned oatmeal.

Chocolate Kissed PB Cookies

Makes 6-8 Servings

Ingredients

Cookie

- ½ c. raw almond butter
- ½ c. raw tahini
- ¾ c. raw agave
- 1 ¼ c. buckwheat, sprouted
- 1 c. coconut flour
- 1 tsp. cinnamon, ground
- ¼ tsp. Himalayan crystal salt

'Chocolate'

- 1 c. raw carob
- ½ c. raw coconut oil
- ½ c. raw liquid sweetener
- ¼ - ¾ c. water

Directions

'Chocolate'

In a bowl, combine the carob, coconut oil, and raw liquid sweetener until evenly mixed and smooth. Add only enough water for it to become thick and creamy--set aside.

Cookie

In a separate bowl, mix almond butter, tahini, agave nectar, and salt until the mixture is creamy and smooth. Set this "peanut butter" aside.

Using a food processor, mix buckwheat, coconut flour, and cinnamon until well combined. Add the peanut butter mixture, and if it is too sticky, use more coconut flour.

Form dough into small balls and place on a nonstick dehydrator sheet. Press thumb into the middle to make an indent. Dehydrate about 2 hours and remove the nonstick dehydrator sheet from the cookies.

Fill the thumbprint with chocolate and continue drying for another 4 to 6 hours or until desired consistency has been achieved.

Cashew Cream

Makes 6-8 Servings

Ingredients

- 2 c. cashews
- 1 ½ c. pure water
- ½ c. raw liquid sweetener
- ¼ inch vanilla bean or raw vanilla powder

Directions

In a blender, combine cashew nuts, orange juice, sweetener, and vanilla. Add just enough water to achieve a very creamy texture.

Note

If no power is available crush cashews in mortar and pestle then add vanilla, sweetener and water as needed for a creamy texture.

Chapter 12 Root Cellar Recipes

How to make delicious recipes from the food you may have in your root cellar. If you don't have a root cellar, use dried vegetables in their place.

Root Salad with Tender Greens

Makes 4-6 Servings

Ingredients

- 4-6 c. baby arugula or other tender greens
- 4 cloves garlic, crushed
- ½ pound parsnips, cut into bite sized pieces
- 2 medium beets, cut into bite sized pieces
- 2 medium turnips, cut into bite sized pieces
- 1 small rutabaga, peeled and cut into bite sized pieces
- 1 tbsp. rosemary
- 4 tbsp. basil
- 1 tsp. black pepper
- 2 tbsp. lemon, juiced
- 5 tbsp. cold pressed olive oil

Directions

Place into a baking dish; parsnips, beets, turnips, and rutabaga. Sprinkle with 3 tablespoons oil, rosemary, garlic, and pepper. Dehydrate for about 5 hours. Stirring occasionally. When ready it should be easy to eat.

Fact

In this book, tender greens refer to greens that are tender to eat. Examples are baby lettuce, arugula, spinach, microgreens, pea greens, sunflower greens, sprouts, and so forth.

Cellar Salad

Makes 6-8 Servings

Ingredients

- 1 ½ c. parsnips, from your root cellar cut into bite sized pieces
- ¾ c. beets, from your root cellar cut into bite sized pieces
- ¾ c. turnips, from your root cellar cut into bite sized pieces
- ¾ c. rutabaga, from your root cellar peeled and cut into bite sized pieces
- 1 tbsp. garlic powder
- ½ c. dried zucchini
- 1 tbsp. dried rosemary
- 4 tbsp. dried basil
- 1 tsp. black pepper
- 2 tbsp. raw apple cider vinegar
- 3 tbsp. cold pressed olive oil
- 4-6 c. sprouts (sunflower greens, kale greens, pea greens, radish greens, etc.)

Directions

Retrieve parsnips, beets, turnips, rutabaga, and sweet potatoes from root cellar. Place parsnips, beets, turnips, rutabaga, and sweet potatoes in a baking dish and sprinkle with 1 ½ tbsp. of oil, rosemary, garlic, and pepper. Marinate for 2 hours.

Just before serving combine sprouts and basil in a large bowl. Toss with vinegar, and remaining 1 ½ tbsp. of oil. Toss with root vegetables and place on serving plate

Note

If you do not have a root cellar, use dried and shredded vegetables; rehydrate with water or liquid.

Unroasted Vegetables with Nuts

Makes 6-8 Servings

Ingredients

- 2 large yams, peeled and cut into bite sized pieces from root cellar
- 3 c. butternut squash, peeled and cut into bite sized pieces from root cellar
- 2 tbsp. pumpkin seeds, soaked
- 1 c. hazelnuts, soaked
- 1 tbsp. onion powder
- 1 tsp. sage
- 1 tsp. marjoram
- 1 tbsp. cold pressed olive oil
- 2 tbsp. lemon powder
- ¼ c. water
- Himalayan crystal salt to taste
- black pepper to taste

Directions

AHEAD OF TIME: Soak hazelnuts and pumpkin seeds overnight in separate bowls, drain off the water.

In a large dish, combine yams and butternut squash with hazelnuts, onion powder, sage, and marjoram.

In a jar, combine the lemon powder, water, and olive oil mix with the squash and nuts. Sprinkle the top with the pumpkin seeds. Dehydrate at 100°F. for about 8 hours, or serve after marinating for 5 hours.

Note

For a more tender bite, shred the yams, pumpkin and butternut squash.

Heavenly Vegetables in Clouds

Makes 6-8 Servings

Ingredients

Vegetables

- 3 c. turnips or jicama, cubed root cellar
- ½ c. baby carrots, dried or from root cellar
- 1 c. peas, freeze dried

Clouds

- 1 ½ c. cashews or macadamia nuts
- ¼ tsp. red chili pepper
- ¼ tsp. kelp
- ¼ tsp. celery seed
- ¼ tsp basil
- ¼ tsp. marjoram
- ¼ tsp. oregano
- ¼ tsp. rosemary
- ¼ tsp. thyme
- 1 tsp. onion powder
- ½ tsp. turmeric
- Himalayan crystal salt to taste
- black pepper to taste
- ½ c. water
- 2 tbsp. lemon powder

Directions

AHEAD of TIME: Soak the lemon powder in water for 20 minutes for lemon juice.

Cut turnip/jicama and carrots and place in a bowl and set aside. Soak dry peas (and if using dried carrots) for 5-10 minutes. Drain water off before adding the jicama.

In a blender combine cashews, lemon juice, red chili pepper, kelp, celery seed, basil, marjoram, oregano, rosemary, thyme, onion powder, turmeric, salt, and pepper mix until creamy--adding water if needed. Pour over prepared vegetables and serve.

Note

If no blender is available, use a mortar and pestle to grind the nuts then add the remaining ingredients.

Apple Pumpkin Stew

Makes 4-6 Servings

Ingredients

- 2 c. pumpkin, peeled, seeded and cubed
- 1 tsp. onions powder
- ¼ c. dried celery, sliced
- 4 medium apples, chopped
- 1 tsp. parsley
- ¼ tsp. pumpkin pie spice
- water as needed
- Himalayan crystal salt to taste
- pepper to taste

Directions

In a blender, combine, pumpkin, 4 apples, parsley, pumpkin pie spice, salt, and pepper until desired consistency is reached. Add water as needed. Should be thick and creamy like a stew base.

Chop 2 apples and place in bowl. Pour soup over apples and dried celery.

Hoppin John

Makes 6-8 Servings

Ingredients

- 1 c. pea greens
- 1 ½ c. wild rice, sprouted
- ¾ c. dried corn
- 1 c. dried red bell pepper, chopped
- ¾ c. dried zucchini, shredded
- 3-4 tsp. onion powder
- 2-4 tsp. garlic powder
- 1 tbsp. lemon powder
- 1 tsp. Himalayan crystal salt
- 1 tsp. thyme
- 1-2 tsp. cold pressed olive oil
- ½ tsp. cayenne pepper
- ½ c. water

Directions

AHEAD OF TIME: Sprout beans, and rice. Grow pea greens

Soak corn, peppers, and zucchini for 20 minutes. Drain the water off and place in a bowl. To the bowl, add sprouted peas, beans, and rice gently mix.

In a jar place, lemon powder, salt, onion powder, garlic powder, thyme, cayenne pepper, water, and olive oil mix well. Toss dressing with vegetables and rice. May garnish with green sprouts.

Moroccan Casserole

Makes 6-8 Servings

Ingredients

Sauce

- 4 tbsp. garlic powder
- 2 tsp. paprika
- ½ tsp. cumin seed, ground
- ¼ tsp. cayenne
- ½ tsp. Himalayan crystal salt
- 4 tbsp. dried parsley
- 1 tsp. lemon powder
- 3 tbsp. raw apple cider vinegar
- 3 tbsp. cold pressed olive oil

Vegetables

- 2 c. jicama, from root cellar, cut into bite sized pieces
- 1 c. dried red bell pepper,
- 1 c. dried yellow bell pepper,
- 1 c. dried orange bell pepper,
- ½ c. dried celery, thinly sliced
- Himalayan crystal salt to taste
- 2 c. dried tomatoes
- 1-2 tbsp. cold pressed olive oil

Directions

Sauce:

For lemon juice soak lemon powder with ¼ c. pure water for 20 minutes in a small bowl. With the lemon juice combine garlic, paprika, cumin, cayenne, salt, parsley and vinegar mix well and set aside.

Vegetables:

In a separate bowl soak bell peppers, celery and tomatoes in water for 20 minutes. Remove the vegetables from water and place in a bowl.

Peel jicama and cut into bite sized pieces. Add jicama and salt to vegetables and mix. Stir in the sauce making sure to coat the vegetables well. May drizzle cold pressed olive oil over the top.

Mom's Apple Pie

Makes 6-8 Servings

Ingredients

Crust
- 1 ½ c. pecans
- ½ c. dates

Filling
- ¼ c. water
- 2 tsp. lemon powder
- 6 c. apples, chopped
- ¼ lemon, juiced
- 1 tsp. nutmeg
- ½ tsp. cloves
- 1 tbsp. vanilla extract
- ¼ tsp. turmeric
- ¼ tsp. Himalayan crystal salt
- ¼ c. raw coconut sugar
- ¼ c. raw almond butter

Crumb Topping
- 1 ½ c. macadamia nuts or cashews
- 1 ½ c. coconut, shredded

Directions

Soak the lemon powder in water for 20 minutes for lemon juice.

Peel, core and chop apples. place them in a bowl with lemon juice and let soak--if it does not cover apples--add more water.

Pie Shell

In a food processor, combine pecans and pitted dates. Combine until well mixed. Press into a pie plate and set aside.

Filling

Remove apples from lemon juice and place in a bowl with nutmeg, cloves, vanilla, turmeric, salt, coconut sugar, and almond butter. Gently mix to cover apples. Place apples into pie shell. Set it aside.

Crumb Topping

In a food processor, coarsely mix macadamia nuts and then slowly add coconut until it's crumbly and well mixed. Sprinkle over top of the pie and let sit for an hour. Serve cold or dehydrate for about 4 hours at 100°F.

Chapter 13
Your Recipes

When fresh vegetables are in season, buy them in bulk and dry them for your storage to enjoy later. Be creative and create your recipes!

The next few pages are for you to make notes of your creations or write down favorite recipes made from your food storage.

Recipe

Serves _____   Source_____

Ingredients

Directions

Recipe

Serves _____   Source_____

Ingredients

Directions

Recipe

Serves _____   Source_____

Ingredients

Directions

Recipe

Serves ____   Source_____

Ingredients

Directions

Recipe

Serves ____   Source_____

Ingredients

Directions

Recipe

Serves _____   Source _____

Ingredients

Directions

Recipe

Serves _____   Source_____

Ingredients

Directions

Recipe

Serves _____   Source_____

Ingredients

Directions

Index

A

Almond Butter 98
Almond Mayo 107
Almond Milk 71
Anytime Breakfast Burrito 92
Apple Carrot Muffins 114
Apple Pie 139
Apple Pumpkin Stew 137

B

Bagels 118
Basic Flax Crackers 108
Basic Pate 96
Basic Seed Cheese 101
Basil 'Ice Cream' 121
Bean Burrito 91
Becky's Cheesecake 123
Beverage
  Almond Milk 71
  Frosty Drink 71
  Happy Juice 55
  Hibiscus Drink 72
  Iron Passion 55
  Peach Mint Lemonade 56
  Rejuvelac 73
  Tropical Smoothie 56
  Watermelon
     Strawberry Drink 57
Black Bottom Coconut Bar 125
Blond Ambition 128
Bread
  Apple Carrot Muffins 114
  Corn Bread 116
  Cranberry Muffins 113
  Garlic Bread 117
  Lemon Poppy Muffins 112
  Nancy's Bread 115
  Raw Bagels 118
Broccoli Soup 58
Brownies 123

C

Cake
  Becky's Cheesecake 123
  Celebration Cake 124
  Crumb Cake 129
  Raspberry Lemon Cake 130
Cardamom Rice 85
Carob Frosting 127
Carob 'Ice Cream' 119
Carob Icing 124
Carrot Ginger Soup 63
Cashew Cream 133
Casserole
  Creamy Mustard
     with Vegetables 87
  Heavenly Vegetables
     in Clouds 137
  Moroccan Casserole 138
Celebration Cake 124
Cellar Salad 135
Chili Stew 70
Chocolate Kissed PB Cookies 133
Cinnamon Rolls 126
Coconut Sugar Bumps 129
Cool Cucumber Soup 70
Corn Bread 116
Crackers
  Basic Flax Crackers 108
  Pizza Crackers 109
  Sesame Crackers 111
  Veggie Crackers 110
Cranberry Muffins 113
Creamed Cauliflower Soup 60
Cream Frosting 121
Creamy Mustard
     with Vegetables 87
Crumb Cake 129

D

Dairy
  Basic Seed Cheese 101
  Basil 'Ice Cream' 121
  Carob 'Ice Cream' 119
  Cashew Cream 133
  'Garlic Butter' 117
  Herbed Vegan Cream Cheese 104
  Honey Butter 117
  Nut Mayo 107

Nut Yogurt 100
Rawmesan 103
Ricotta Cheese Sauce 100
Sour Cream 105
Spicy Cheese 106
Vegan Feta Cheese 102
Yogurt 100
Dirty Rice 84

E

Eggless Salad 76

F

Falafel Patties 89
Fiesta Dressing 74
Flax Crackers 108
Frosty Drink 71
Fruit Compote 99
Fudge 128

G

Garden Soup 58
Garlic Bread 117
'Garlic Butter' 117
Greek Dressing 74
Ground Meatless 90

H

Happy Juice 55
Heavenly Vegetables
   in Clouds 137
Herbed Almond Spread 97
Herbed Vegan Cream Cheese 104
Hibiscus Drink 72
Honey Butter 117
Hoppin John 138

I

Iron Passion 55
Italian Dressing 75
Italian Tomato Soup 67

K

Kale Burger 88
Kale Soup 68
Kamut Salad with Vinaigrette 79

L

Lasagna 90
Layered Taco Salad 81
Lemon Dill Dressing 74
Lemon Pie 131
Lemon Poppy Muffins 112
Lemon Rice 85

M

Mayo 107
Mexican Vegetable Soup 65
Microgreen Salad 78
Microgreen Salad with
   Lime Vinaigrette 78
Mixed Sprout Salad 81
Mom's Apple Pie 139
Moroccan Casserole 138
Mung Sprouts Salad 83

N

Nacho Cheese 103
Nancy's Bread 115
Nut Mayo 107
Nut Yogurt 100

O

Oatmeal Cookies 132
Olive Pizza 95

P

Parsnip Chowder 69
Pate 96
Peach Mint Lemonade 56
Peanut Butter Bars 127
Philly Pizza 94
Pizza Crackers 109

R

Rabbits Carrot Soup 61
Raspberry Lemon Cake 130
Raw Bagels 118
Rawmesan 103
Rejuvelac 73
Rice
   Cardamom Rice 85
   Dirty Rice 84
   Hoppin John 138

Lemon Rice 85
Unroasted Vegetables
    with Nuts 136
Warm Mexi-Rice 87
Wild Jambalaya 86
Wild Rice and
    Microgreen Salad 82
Wild Rice Chowder 84
Ricotta Cheese Sauce 100
Root Salad with
    Tender Greens 134

S

Salad
  Eggless Salad 76
  Kamut Salad with
      Vinaigrette 79
  Layered Taco Salad 81
  Microgreen Salad 78
  Microgreen Salad with Lime
      Vinaigrette 78
  Mixed Sprout Salad 81
  Mung Sprouts Salad 83
  Sprout Salad 77
  'Tuna' Salad 80
  Wild Rice and
      Microgreen Salad 82
Salad Dressing
  Fiesta Dressing 74
  Greek Dressing 74
  Italian Dressing 75
  Tahini Sauce 99
Seed Cheese 101
Sesame
  Tahini 99
Sesame Crackers 111
Soft Gingerbread Cookies 122
Soup
  Apple Parsnip Soup 62
  Broccoli Soup 58
  Carrot Ginger Soup 63
  Chili Stew 70
  Cool Cucumber Soup 70
  Corn Chowder 62
  Creamed Cauliflower Soup 60
  Garden Soup 58

  Italian Tomato Soup 67
  Kale Soup 68
  Mexican Vegetable Soup 65
  Parsnip Chowder 69
  Rabbits Carrot Soup 61
  Sprouted Soup 83
  Taco Soup 59
  Vegetable 'Noodle' Soup 64
  Vegetable Soup Base 64
Sour Cream 105
Sprouted Pilaf 92
Sprouted Soup 83
Sprout Salad 77
Strawberry 'Ice Cream' 120
Stroganoff 98
Stuffing 96
Sunflower Beans 91

T

Taco Pizza 93
Taco Soup 59
Tahini 99
Tahini Sauce 99
Tropical Smoothie 56
'Tuna' Salad 80

U

Unroasted Vegetables
    with Nuts 136

V

Vegan Feta Cheese 102
Vegetable 'Noodle' Soup 64
Vegetable Soup Base 64
Veggie Crackers 110

W

Warm Mexi-Rice 87
Watermelon Strawberry Drink 57
Wheat Salad with Vinaigrette 79
Wild Jambalaya 86
Wild Rice and Microgreen Salad 82
Wild Rice Chowder 84

Y

Yummy Oatmeal Cookies 132

About the Author

Kachina Choate, a long-time vegetarian, ironically didn't like vegetables. She stood up one day and said, "I'm tired of eating food that tastes like twigs, weeds, and Styrofoam--there has to be a better way."

Since then, she has been creating and serving healthy food to her unsuspecting friends who--when they find out the food is raw & fresh, have said, "I can't believe I ate something healthy... and liked it!"

She is the author of In the Season Thereof, 101 ½ Raw Zucchinis and What to do With Them, Pumpkins Do Grow on Trees, Thriving on Plant-Based Food Storage, The Beautiful Soup and Salad Book, The Pizza Book and Kachina Summer Bear Recipe Card Collection.

She began her natural, unprocessed, raw food journey in 2002, and as a result, has recovered from depression and kicked a pernicious sugar addiction. She loves to travel and teach healthy food that tastes delicious.

She started Summer Bear Life Balance Education, a non-profit organization to help people achieve health and balanced life.

Website: SummerBear.org; Facebook/SummerBearLifeBalance; Instagram: summer_bear_org

Pinterest: dollkachina/raw-food-wfpb-food-storage-by- summerbearorg dollkachina/kachina-summer-bears-raw-foods

www.ingramcontent.com/pod-product-compliance
Lightning Source LLC
Chambersburg PA
CBHW041128110526
44592CB00020B/2726